The Birds of Blashford Lakes

Simon Woolley

Dedicated to the memory of Ron "Chunky" King

FICEDULA
an independent imprint

First published 2013
Second edition 2021

Ficedula Press
The Willows
Snails Lane
Blashford BH24 3PG, UK

ISBN-13: 979-8-4678-7498-2

Contents

Acknowledgments

First, thanks must go to the many observers who have contributed records via the Hampshire Ornithological Society and its forerunner, the Ornithological Section of the Hampshire Field Club, over nine decades.

I must thank several individuals personally, however. Without their help, this publication would not have been anything like complete. **John Clark** and **Keith Betton** provided electronic data sets and Hampshire Bird Reports respectively, and John also commented on the status accounts since the 1980s. **Bob Chapman**, Warden of the Reserve in recent years also commented widely and contributed several unpublished records.

Mike Read allowed me access to his records (some of which have not appeared elsewhere before) from an otherwise poorly recorded period. **Ian Sibsey**, **Alan Lewis**, **Rob Hume**, **Kevin Sayer** and **Andy Lester** (to whom I shall refer, to their embarrassment, as "the Blashford big guns", along with Bob and John) also contributed records and fine-tuned some of my comments. All errors and misinterpretations are, of course, my responsibility.

Thanks also to **Mike Read**, **Carl Chapman** and **Keith Betton** for use of their truly excellent photographs.

Finally, I must thank my wife, **Julia Casson**, for putting up with hours of my 'nerdy' investigations of the precise status of not very rare birds at a not very spectacular local patch. This book is dedicated to her, and to my dogs and cats, who have eaten hardly any of the birds of Blashford Lakes, and no rare ones whatsoever.

Blashford Lakes

The area known here as **Blashford Lakes** is a collection of disused and flooded gravel pits in the upper Avon Valley, south-west Hampshire. Formerly part of the Somerley Estate, the land was largely given over to the Royal Air Force from 1941-52. RAF Ibsley was home to Spitfires, Hurricanes and various other marques (including many USAF aircraft) during the Second World War and the period immediately afterwards.

The only obvious remnant of this time is the abandoned control tower beside Mockbeggar Lake, although a few sections of runway are still visible. The so-called "lichen heath" sections of the Reserve are underlain by expanses of impermeable concrete from this period.

Following the departure of the RAF, the airfield was used for a time for motor racing, prior to the commencement of gravel extraction in the 1950s. Today, about 30 lakes occupy these former workings. While gravel extraction continues west of the A338, the area treated here is, after more than 50 years, free from industrial activity. The older lakes tend to be deeper and less productive for birds than the newer ones, which have been restored more sympathetically.

Water levels vary within and between years, sometimes rather substantially. This has at least three major effects on the avifauna of the area:

1) High water levels are correlated with widespread **flooding in the Avon Valley**, and consequently **higher than average numbers of wildfowl** in the area in winter;

2) High water levels tend to make less accessible or to **reduce the supply of various aquatic foodplants** (especially *Elodea canadensis*), thus **suppressing the numbers of Coot and Gadwall**;

3) Low water levels during passage periods **expose various shorelines and islands**, making the area **more attractive to waders**, or at least make any such species more conspicuous and more prone to stay for extended periods.

Definition of the area treated

The area treated in this review is circumscribed by **Gorley Road to the east, the A338 to the west, the suburbs of Ringwood (Poulner) to the south and Mockbeggar Lane to the north** (see maps and aerial photos from page 11). However, for reasons of completeness, and because most of the wildfowl counts include these waters, **Somerley Lakes, Ibsley North pit** and **Hucklesbrook gravel pits** are all <u>included</u>. The Avon Valley *sensu stricto*, Harbridge and Ibsley water meadows are all excluded. They are of great importance for birds, and have produced some exciting records of rarities over the years. But a line must be drawn.

Habitats for birds

Open water covers 80-90% of the area treated here. Not surprisingly, the Lakes are best known for their waterbirds, waders and other birds which use the open waters to rest, feed and roost. However, there are also other significant habitats. **Gravel shorelines and islands** are very important for nesting and roosting waterbirds and waders, as well as breeding Little Ringed Plovers, Lapwing, Oystercatchers and gulls. **Short-cropped grassland** supports grazing geese and Wigeon. **Early successional willow carr**, such as near the Lapwing Hide, holds breeding and roosting Reed Buntings, roosting Pied Wagtails and winter thrushes. **Mature carr** is important for winter finches, occasional Woodcock and woodpeckers. Small fringing patches of **mature deciduous woodland** support woodpeckers, owls and a multitude of passerines. There are also patches of **coniferous trees** (mostly Scots Pine), **scrub** and **eutrophic swamp**. Two **gravel-bedded streams** run east-west, notably the internationally important Dockens Water, an "oligomesotrophic" tributary of the Hampshire Avon, which supports trout and salmon, Brook Lampreys and Kingfishers!

Data sources and data quality

The primary sources for this report have been **Hampshire Bird Reports (*HBR*)** produced annually by the **Hampshire Ornithological Society (*HOS*)** since its formation in 1978, and prior to that (with records available back to 1958) by the **Ornithological Section of the Hampshire Field Club**. In addition, Clark & Eyre's **"Birds of Hampshire" (*BoH*)**, 1993, has been of great help. A very few blanks have been filled with the help of the BTO's ***Wetland and Estuary Birds Survey* (WEBS)** reports, and their variously named predecessors.

More recently, with the advent of electronic data submission and recording, other sources have been available. The County Bird Recorder, **Keith Betton**, made available machine-readable scans or electronic versions of all HBRs since 1959. **John Clark** extracted all COBRA database records from 1992 to the present. In addition, the *GoingBirding* website, established by **Marek Walford** in 2009, is now an excellent source of up-to-the-minute data.

Sadly, many older records have probably been lost or subsumed within aggregated datasets. These records may have been submitted accurately, but published under headings such as "Avon Valley" or

"Ibsley area". It is thus impossible to extract precise details for some records without recourse to excessively difficult scouring of old paper records. Nonetheless, I am confident that not too much detail, and not too many significant records, have been lost in this way. Equally, significant records are still "lost" to *HOS* and the *HBR* by way of observers logging sightings on *GoingBirding*, but not submitting the reports formally. An *ad hoc* approach has been taken to such reports, and several are included in this report. For very rare species, the caveat of "reported" is generally included next to such "unofficial" but probably good records. Square brackets are used for probably sound but unofficial records.

A few species (e.g. Tree Sparrow) have certainly been recorded in the area at some time, but no precise data exist. They have been included with notes to this effect. A very few species have also been included on a putative, "square-bracketed" basis, again using the author's skill and perhaps dubious judgment, in an Appendix.

<u>Observer coverage</u>

There are dated records for the area since the mid-1950s, but intensive watching did not begin until the 1970s. Waders and wildfowl have been especially well-recorded since. Watching was intensive in the 1980s, and still more since about 2000. Access to the Lakes has not always been as straightforward as it is now. Moreover, the habitat is in a constant state of flux, making the area at times more, at times less attractive to both birds and birders. Some very good wader habitat, especially, has been lost as a result of certain pits being flooded, but equally more waterfowl habitat is available than ever before.

Some measure of the intensity of coverage may be drawn from the graph below, which shows the number of *records* (not absolute numbers) of "notifiable rarities" detected per year during 1958-2012. These include (a) **bona fide national/regional rarities** (e.g. Long-tailed Skua, Long-billed Dowitcher, Ring-billed Gull), (b) **genuine local rarities** (e.g. Firecrest, Hawfinch, Crossbill), (c) **substantially under-recorded species** (e.g. Tree Pipit, Marsh Tit), and (d) **probably once frequent and now locally rare and individually recorded birds** (e.g. Turtle Dove, Yellowhammer).

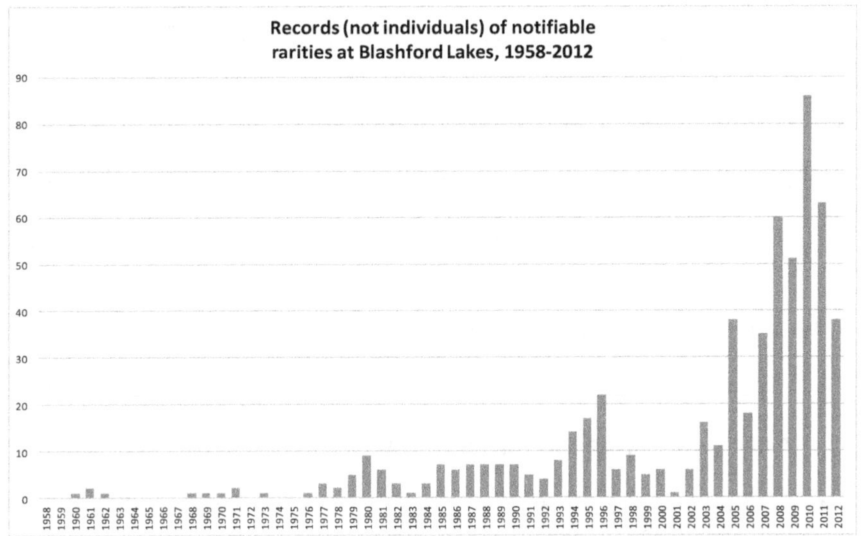

Blashford Lakes has seen an upsurge in the number of notable records submitted in recent years, mostly in line with the "opening up" of the site to birders by the establishment of the Blashford Lakes Partnership. The peak year of 2010 was a superb one, seeing records of such "megas" as Glossy Ibis, Long-tailed Skua and Long-eared Owl, a near-complete suite of passage waders, rare gulls and wildfowl, and some other highly unexpected visitors. 2010 was also the year when Blashford Lakes entered and **won the "Large Wetland" Bird Count category of the *BTO - EDF Energy Business Bird Challenge*, recording a spectacular 169 species.** This was a happy coincidence, and probably spurred even better coverage than usual.

Site names and nomenclature

There is much confusion over the names given to different areas of the Blashford Lakes complex, for a variety of reasons. First, different interest groups call different areas by different names. For example:

- **Snails Lake** = Roach Pit to anglers
- **Spinnaker Lake** (the sailors' name) = Blashford Lake (*sensu stricto*) in some old bird documents
- **Ellingham Lake** is widely known as the "waterski pit", a name which also used to apply to **Ivy Lake** when uses were differently allocated!

I have tried as far as possible to stick to the currently used "birders' names" for the various areas, as per the current names in *HBR*s.

One particular source of trouble is that, with a constantly evolving habitat and new pits being dug and then filled with water, what constitutes "X Lake" or "Y Water" has been up for debate. The prime example of this is "Mockbeggar Lake", which now strictly refers to the north-easternmost lake, and is poor for waders, having few feeding opportunities around its densely-vegetated edges. However, as a glance at the Systematic List will show, "Mockbeggar Lake" used to supply the majority of really good bird records, especially of passage waders and terns. First, the habitat has clearly changed drastically. But the water body now known as **Ibsley Water** was, even when it was a chain of disconnected pits, often known as "Mockbeggar Lake" (or "Lakes", a name which was also for used for the *entire site*!).

This knot will never be fully unravelled, and it does not ultimately matter. In the Systematic List I have used the name under which individual records were noted in *HBR* or elsewhere unless there is a good reason not to. For example, "Blashford Lake" has been converted to "Spinnaker Lake" throughout. Where the record was noted as being at "Blashford Lakes", I have made no attempt to second guess exactly where the birds were.

Perhaps surprisingly, there are rather few "site specific" or "birders'" place names which apply to specific spots at Blashford Lakes! I, for one, would encourage readers to start thinking up and using some! My personal coining is "Teal Bay", the area in the north-east corner of Ivy Lake which cannot be observed from either of the Ivy Lake hides, and only partly from the northern screen on the Ivy/Rockford path. It is a favourite haunt of (guess what!) Teal and occasional Smew.

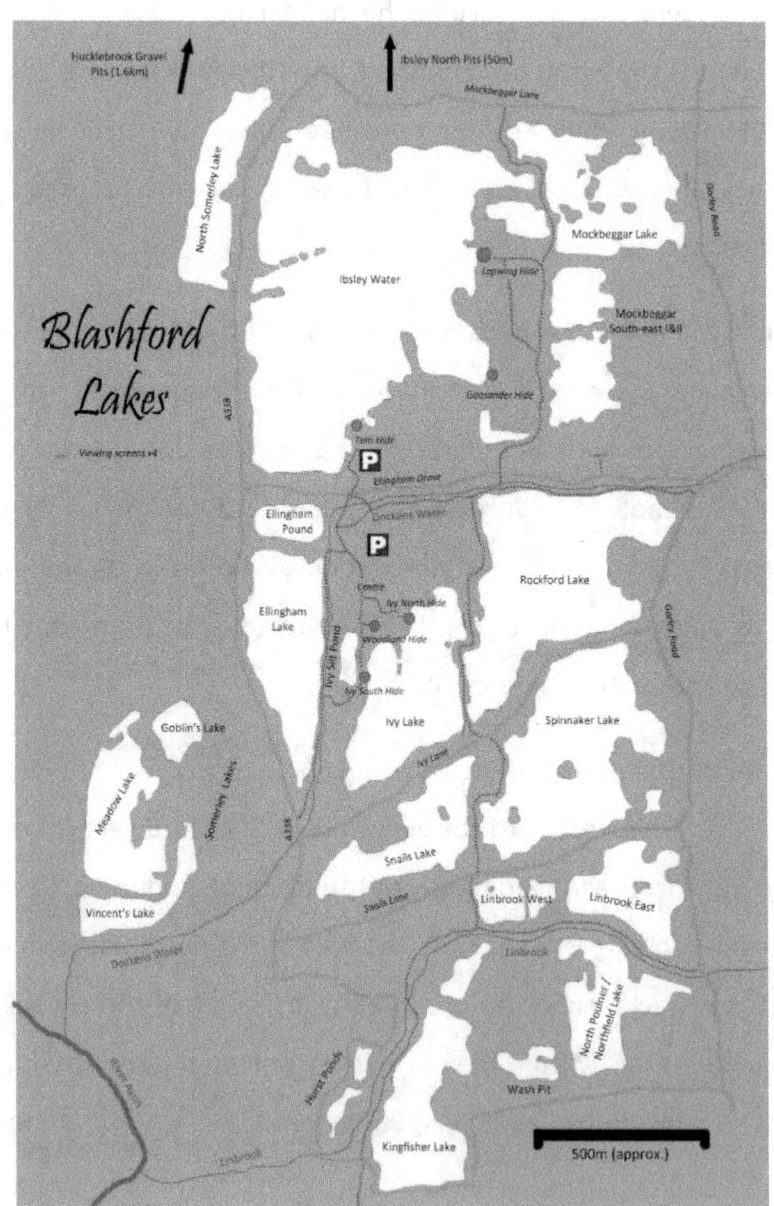

Hucklebrook Gravel Pits (1.6km)
Ibsley North Pits (50m)
Mockbeggar Lane
North Somerley Lake
Gorley Road
Mockbeggar Lake
Ibsley Water
Lapwing Hide
Mockbeggar South-east I & II
Blashford Lakes
A338
Goosander Hide
Tern Hide
P
Ellingham Drove
Ellingham Pound
Dockens Water
Viewing screens x4
P
Centre
Rockford Lake
Ivy North Hide
Ellingham Lake
Woodland Hide
Ivy Silt Pond
Ivy South Hide
Gorley Road
Goblin's Lake
Ivy Lake
Spinnaker Lake
Meadow Lake
Somerley Lakes
Ivy Lane
A338
Snails Lake
Vincent's Lake
Snails Lane
Linbrook West
Linbrook East
Dockens Water
Linbrook
River Avon
North Poulner / Northfield Lake
Hurst Ponds
Wash Pit
Linbrook
Kingfisher Lake
500m (approx.)

Ibsley Water
Lapwing Hide
Ibsley North
Mockbeggar Lake

Ellingham Lake and Pound
Woodland Hide
Ivy North Hide
Ibsley Water
Tern Hide
Ivy Lake
Rockford Lake
Spinnaker Lake

North Poulner Lake
Linbrook East
Kingfisher Lake
Linbrook West
Spinnaker Lake
Snails Lane fields
(now mostly dry)
Snails Lake
Ivy Lake

Rockford Lake
Spinnaker Lake
Snails Lake
Linbrook East
Linbrook West
Kingfisher
Lake (north)
North Poulner Lake

The birding year at Blashford Lakes

It makes sense to describe the birding year as starting not in January, but in late winter, just as wildfowl numbers start to decline, and as the very first spring migrants appear. What follows is a description of what would be a *very* good year at Blashford Lakes!

March

Goldeneye numbers generally peak about now, as passage birds heading north stop off at the Lakes, often displaying vigorously. Might they stay and breed one day? Equally, there is considerable turnover among the often large concentrations of **Coot** and other waterbirds. The former can sometimes be heard calling as they fly high overhead at night, making a bizarre trumpeting call. There is always a chance of an errant duck: the Lakes' only **Velvet Scoter** was found in March. **Shelduck** numbers often pick up in March as well, ahead of dispersal to inland breeding sites, although counts are lower now than a few years ago. Only a very few will stay and breed on site. **Black-necked Grebes** are not infrequent, and may stay into April, by which time they will be looking simply superb! The first passerine summer migrants are generally **Blackcaps** and **Chiffchaffs** from mid-month. They coincide with the vanguard of **Sand Martins** and sometimes **Wheatears**, which almost invariably both turn up at Ibsley Water. Suitable weather may well bring a couple of **Little Gulls**, for a few hours at least. It would be worth keeping an ear open from the calls and drumming of **Lesser Spotted Woodpecker** just now. While rare and far from regular, this is the peak time for detecting a potential breeding pair. Also worth looking for are **Rock Pipits**. While there are very few records, this is the peak time, and any present might just be of the Scandinavian form, *littoralis*.

April

This month often flatters to deceive: spring is here, but chill winds still blow, and the watcher may find himself watching flocks of **Sand Martins** or **LRPs** in a blizzard! Nonetheless, migrant numbers are building all the time, with decent arrivals of **hirundines** guaranteed by mid-month, perhaps an early **Swift** before the 20th of the month, and any remaining winter wildfowl looking superb and getting decidedly frisky. By the end of the month, all the summer migrants will be in (perhaps having featured a cheeky temporarily singing **Nightingale, Wood Warbler** or **Whitethroat**. None of these breeds at the Lakes). All but the last straggling wildfowl will have gone. The **Little Ringed Plovers, Lapwings** and **Oystercatchers** will have built nests and be incubating, but Foxes often scupper their chances of breeding success. The last week of April is the peak time for the sharp-eyed to pick out an **Arctic Tern** among the more numerous **Common Terns**. **Sandwich** and **Little Terns** are much rarer visitors, but this is the time to look. Little Gulls are seen regularly in this month, and three of the four most recent Aprils have turned up a **Bonaparte's Gull**, and they were all different birds! Eyes should be to the skies for migrating **Ospreys**, and perhaps more: the only two **Black Kites** were seen in April 2011 and 2016 .

May

May can be a real red-letter month. **Hobbies** are likely over Ibsley Water, although numbers are lower than a few years ago. They might be joined by some **Little Gulls** and/or **Black Terns**, but probably only briefly. This is the time for Arctic waders. **Dunlin** are the most likely, but scarcer visitors might include **Turnstone**, **Bar-tailed Godwit**, **Whimbrel**, **Knot**, **Grey Plover** (very rarely) or even **Temminck's Stint**.. There might be the chance of a *really* rare visitor too: **Red-footed Falcon**, **White Stork**, **Black-winged Stilt**, **Collared Pratincole** and **Whiskered Tern** have all been recorded in May. A potential mega-month! More prosaically, **Sedge Warblers** will be incubating, **Yellow Wagtails** will be passing through in, sadly, ever-decreasing numbers, and the Ibsley Water **Sand Martin** colony will be in full swing.

June

This is the time when many birders pack away their telescopes and switch to plants or insects, and indeed the Lakes area will be burgeoning and humming with both, but there is always the chance of a sting in spring's ornithological tail. Very late migrant waders are probably from the most northerly breeding populations, so the very observant might just confirm that some of the **Ringed Plovers** are of the form *tundrae*, and the very rare June **Little Stints** are probably north- rather than south-bound. A bizarre (and the Lakes' only) record concerns a **Kentish Plover** in June. And the only two records of **Red-necked Phalarope** have come in recent Junes. Never give up!

July

Almost as soon as spring has finished, autumn has arrived, with southbound **Green** and **Common Sandpipers**, **Dunlin** and other waders possible. Very oddly, one of the Lakes' six **Common Scoters** has been found in June, and another two in July! And the first **Cattle Egret** and **Purple Heron** have turned up in July, too. Clearly, anything is possible on balmy, and especially hazy summer days. Midsummer thunderstorms can also 'ground' waders and terns. July is also not too early for the first returning **Ospreys**, and this is a great time for **Crossbills**, assuming their local populations are at reasonable levels, or an irruption is in progress. This is also the time when **Great White Egrets** usually reappear.

August

By now, waders are well on the move. **Greenshank**, **Ruff** and even scarcities like **Spotted Redshank** are all possible. By mid-month, autumn migration of passerines is in full swing, with newly-fledged **Redstarts**, **Whitethroats**, **Sedge** and **Reed Warblers** all likely to be encountered, albeit in small numbers, and **Tree Pipits** could be detected in flight. Fledged **Common Terns** will be making their presence noisily felt over Ivy and Rockford Lakes, in particular, and are sometimes joined by migrating, moulting **Black Terns**. At least a couple of **Ospreys** are usually picked up in August, with probably more to come next month. The raptor-aware might pick up a **Honey-buzzard** wandering from the New Forest, too. This is a great time to find a **Garganey**, incidentally. And try beating the only Lakes records of **Gannet** or **Ring-necked Parakeet**: both were observed on sunny August days!

September

Autumn is really here now, and with wildfowl numbers starting to build, and lots of fledglings still hanging about, the Lakes are busy, and there is a sense of expectation among birders. What will this

September bring? Past years have seen **Grey Phalarope, Long-tailed Skua, Fulmar, Glossy Ibis, Pectoral Sandpiper** (twice) and **White-winged Black Tern**, and perhaps closer scrutiny of passerines would yield some more **Grasshopper Warblers, Pied Flycatchers** or **Whinchats**?

October

This is a month to make the coastal rarity hunter's pulse quicken, and Blashford has had some "right megas" (at least on the local scale) in October too over the years. Try 40 **Brent Geese**, a flock of nine **Glossy Ibises, Ring Ouzel, Bearded Tit, Wryneck, Shore Lark, Ring-billed Gull** or **Long-billed Dowitcher** on for size! **Lesser Scaup** finally fell one late October day in 2017. More significantly, the last remnants of wader migration will be in evidence (perhaps including a late **Little Stint**), and wildfowl numbers will be rising rapidly. The gull roost, such a feature of recent autumn and winter evenings on Ibsley Water, will be growing apace. **Lesser Black-backed Gulls** predominate at this stage, probably including plenty of *intermedius* birds, and perhaps the odd individual suggesting *fuscus*? **Yellow-legged Gulls** should be about too, mixed in with lots of **Black-headed Gulls**, a few **Mediterranean Gulls**, and maybe a **Caspian** or **Iceland Gull**. In October 2017, Hampshire's second **Franklin's Gull** lingered.

The first **Bitterns** might appear, but wintering birds are not usually in until mid-December.

November

Winter's chills take hold from now on, and as the nights draw in, the birder's attention switches increasingly to wildfowl, although late **Ruff**, occasional parties of **Black-tailed Godwit**, hunting **Peregrines** and errant raptors such as **Hen** or **Marsh Harrier**, or even **Merlin**, might put in appearances. One might even find a **Black Redstart**, and November 17th is "the" date to find an **Avocet**, it would appear! This also appears to be peak time for finding a diver, most likely a **Great Northern**, and other November oddities have included **Pale-bellied Brent Goose, Eider, Little Auk, Grey Phalarope, Slavonian Grebe, Leach's Petrel, Ring-necked Duck** and several **Long-tailed Ducks**. But the ever-growing herds of diving and dabbling ducks really catch the eye. **Gadwall** will soon peak, perhaps at over 1000, **Shoveler** are piling in (though probably not on the scale of the winter of 2012/13), **Pintail** numbers are on the up, and decent flocks of **Teal**, **Wigeon** and **Tufted Duck** will be on show. **Pochard** numbers are still respectable, but much lower than they once were.

December

With Christmas and the new (calendar) year beckoning, non-waterbird interest has all but dried up. One of the very few **Spoonbill** records was in December, rather oddly, and other rarities have included **Red-necked Grebe**, **Ferruginous Duck**, **Arctic Skua**, **Kittiwake**, **Ring-billed Gull** (now regular, despite declining to near official rarity status, nationally speaking) both **Long-eared** and **Short-eared Owls**, and **Snow Bunting**. The gull roost is probably at peak numbers by now, although the **Lesser Black-backs** will probably all be British *graellsi* birds by now. An errant **Caspian**, **Mediterranean** or even a "white-winged" gull are all possible, but will need careful picking out from thousands of **LBBGs** and **Black-headed Gulls** in the fading light of dusk. **Coot** numbers generally peak now, at around 2000 birds, and the wintering duck cohorts are all but complete, barring a cold spell in the new year. If cold weather does take a grip, it's a great time to find **Woodcock**, and maybe **Hawfinch** or even **Waxwing**, if it is an invasion year for the latter. **Redwing** and sometimes **Fieldfare** are present in numbers, and the **Reed Bunting** and **Pied Wagtail** roosts make for good entertainment. Other passerines include **Siskin**, **Lesser Redpoll** and **Brambling**, and wintering **Bitterns** may be on view from Ivy North Hide. **Marsh Harriers** are seen almost year-round these days, but mid-winter is a good time to watch them hunting wildfowl. Other raptors such as **Goshawk** are worth checking for, and a wild **White-tailed Eagle** turned up in December 2018. In recent winters, there have been three winter **Yellow-browed Warblers**, with two more in October.

January

A happy new year for all but the birds: a hard, cold snap in January can bring great rewards at Blashford Lakes. **Smew** used to be almost annual, but are now very rare. Forced movements of wildfowl can and do carry more unusual visitors with them, such as **Barnacle Goose** (but are they ever wild?), **Green-winged Teal** (twice), **Red-crested Pochard**, **Ring-necked Duck**, semi-regular **Scaup**, **Slavonian Grebe** and even a very unseasonal **Grey Phalarope**. Occasional **Red-breasted Mergansers** do turn up on Ibsley Water, joining the much commoner **Goosanders**. The latter were distinctly rare until recent years, but their winter roost numbers can now sometimes exceed 200 birds. If there are any **Bewick's Swans** (or even less likely, **White-fronted Geese**) in the Avon Valley, this is a good month to look out for them dropping in to roost. Sadly, the days of hundreds of each roosting have long gone. But more than anything, it is the overall peak month for waterbird numbers. 6-7000 birds are likely to be down on the water all day, joined by up to 10,000 gulls at night.

Where else in Hampshire can you find an inland site with almost 20,000 birds to look at, apart from the odd rubbish tip! The large gull roost may well contain a vagrant gem: January 2018 turned up Hampshire's first **Thayer's Gull**, and the site's only **Glaucous Gull** was found on New Year's Day 2015. A **Water Pipit** or two are likely around the margins of Ibsley Water.

February

Unless that "January" cold snap comes late, February is probably the nadir of the birder's year. Migration has yet to start, and while there are still plenty of wildfowl to check, and maybe the odd rarity to see (**American Wigeon**, **Tundra Bean Goose**, **Black-throated Diver**), excitement is usually limited to small numbers of wintering **Green Sandpipers**, and maybe the odd **Common Sandpiper**, and passerine activity around the Woodland Hide. Growing **Lesser Redpoll** numbers may signal the arrival of a **"Mealy" Common Redpoll** or two, but the odds must be against another **"Greenland" Redpoll**, like the one which appeared in 2009! **Brambling** numbers will soon grow, ahead of the spring departure, and birds might even be heard singing in the alders on bright days. But the wheel is turning, and the year with it, and those **Goldeneye** numbers are just starting to get ready to peak once more. Here comes spring again!

The systematic list

This list covers all 241 species which have occurred in a wild state at Blashford Lakes (i.e. BOU Categories A and C). A lenient view has been taken of Snow Geese and Barnacle Geese, which are (respectively) wholly and at least largely accounted for by escapes and feral birds. Appendices list species which are suspected or have been plausibly reported, but for which no substantiated records exist, a few which *may* have occurred in the area in the 19th century, and assorted escapes. Species names and order follow the 2020 BOURC British List. Records are complete to 2020, with a few records to Sep 2021 also included.

A note on ageing terminology

The terms "juvenile" and "first-winter" are often used inaccurately or wrongly. Where a bird was undoubtedly a juvenile, seen shortly after fledging (e.g. Ruff, Garganey), I have used that term, but where there is any doubt, and certainly in the case of birds with identifiable "immature" plumages after their first year (e.g. gulls), I have used the terms "1cy", "2cy" etc., meaning "first/second calendar year". There are confusing possibilities when a bird shifts from being a 1cy to a 2cy on Jan 1st, but this seems preferable to second-guessing whether a transitional "first-winter/first-summer" is either or neither of those things! A special case arises with a high Arctic breeder such as Iceland Gull, which technically retains its juvenile plumage throughout its first winter. I have used the term "juvenile" advisedly in that case.

Brent Goose   *Branta bernicla*
A very rare winter visitor and passage migrant.

Twelve records of 67 birds.

1985 Ivy Lake	3, Feb 3rd
1986	Apr 30th
1987 Mockbeggar Lake	10 (7 1cys), Dec 26th
2005 Ibsley Water	40 flew south, Oct 29th
2008 Rockford Lake	Dec 14th
2014 Ibsley Water	Feb 27th
2016 Ibsley Water	Oct 5th; 4 *hrota*, Nov 22nd
2017 Ibsley Water	6, Sep 25th; Dec 5th
2018 Ibsley Water	Dec 31st-Jan 1st 2019
2020 Ibsley Water	Feb 4th; Mar 14th

This species is very rare inland, and the 2005 record is little short of astonishing! Records are perhaps most probable around departure/arrival time for this species, when flocks are orientating themselves from/to their coastal wintering areas. The close coincidence of the 2016 records of both Dark-bellied and Light-bellied Brents (the latter the first ever in the Avon Valley) are remarkable. Also *cf.* Eider on the latter date!

Red-breasted Goose   *Branta ruficollis*
An extremely rare winter visitor.

Birds have occurred in the Avon Valley on three occasions, and it is assumed that at least one of them visited the Lakes, at least once!

1967	Jan 18th-Feb 9th
1969	Jan 11th-19th
1983	Dec 27th-Jan 15th 1984

Canada Goose
Branta canadensis

A common resident.

The first published record is of 20 on Kingfisher Lake on Feb 3rd 1968, and a count of 51 was made there on Dec 19th 1970. By 1977, numbers had built up, reaching 306 in Dec, and several hundred have been in the area ever since. 500 were counted in Aug 2001, and an all-time high was reached in Nov 2011, when 534 were counted. This was beaten in 2014 (575, June) and approached again in 2015 (512, June). A Ringwood-Fordingbridge count of 592 in Sep 2020 suggests numbers are no lower today. A bird resembling one of the "small races", now widely split as Cackling (Canada) Goose (*B. hutchinsii*) was seen at Ibsley Water on July 24th 1999, Apr 22nd 2000 and Aug 25th 2001 and another was present on Dec 14th 2010. These were not regarded as wild birds.

Barnacle Goose
Branta leucopsis

A rare visitor, probably mostly from feral populations. Natural vagrancy is not impossible.

About eighteen records of 26-31 birds.

1982 various lakes	up to four, "throughout the year"
1994 St Ivel Lake	two, May 20th
1995 Rockford Lake	July 2nd
1996 various lakes	June 19th; Aug 12th-16th and 31st; 3 dates during Oct 12th-Jan 26th 1997
1997 various lakes	intermittently, Aug 16th-Feb 8th 1998
1999 various lakes	July 18th; Nov 28th
2007 Ibsley Water	4, May 17th and June 10th
2009 Ibsley Water	Feb 27th; 3, Oct 31st; 1, arrived with Bewick's Swans, Dec 20th, and suspected of being wild

2010 Ibsley Water	Jan 18th and 21st;
	Aug 7th
2012 Ibsley Water	5, Feb 2nd-26th
2013 Ibsley Water	3, Jan 20th-22nd, 2 still present, 23rd -27th
2016 Ibsley Water	Aug 14th – with an Emperor Goose *qv.*
2020 Ibsley Water	July 1st

While most (if not all) of the earlier records almost certainly refer to feral birds from the small and now almost defunct Hampshire population, more recent records may well be of wild birds, or perhaps more likely derive from other British feral populations.

Snow Goose   *Anser caerulescens*

A rare feral visitor, which has hybridised locally.

No *truly* wild Snow Geese have ever been recorded at Blashford Lakes, but the species formerly bred in a wild state in Hampshire. However, one bird was "at Ibsley" during Jan 1st-Apr 14th 1972, and from Oct 12th to the end of that year at least. Whether it was seen at the Lakes is not known. Two blue-phase birds were present in the area in 1981. In 1997, one was seen semi-regularly in the summer, and in 1998, it was at Ibsley Water on Mar 28th and from July 11th-Sep 30th. In 2001, it nested successfully with a Greylag Goose at Somerley Lakes. The same pair bred again in 2003 and 2004, and since then, various hybrids have been seen. Whether a claim of a blue-phase Snow Goose at Ibsley Water on Feb 20th 2005 refers to such a bird is unclear. One was seen on Aug 23rd 2014, but not confirmed as a "pure" Snow Goose.

Greylag Goose   *Anser anser*

A common resident and visitor, from feral populations.

Until the early 1970s, this species was essentially unknown in the Avon Valley, but its status has changed drastically and explosively. In 1973, one was reportedly "at Ibsley from Jan 3rd-Mar 3rd, but this probably did not refer to the Lakes, and in 1974 a "Game Conservancy free-flying flock" was in residence nearby. Consistent records for the Lakes do not appear until 1984, when as many as 370 were present in autumn. Despite frequent breeding at the Lakes (e.g. 2 pairs in 2001, 4 pairs in 2009, but probably breeding annually) and nearby, this level was not reached again until 2009, when 381 were recorded in Sep. In 2010, an exceptional 520 on Nov 23rd comprised the annual and all-time maximum. Numbers fell back to a more typical level in 2011, prior to a refreshed growth in numbers: 450, Dec 2013 (a year when 7 pairs bred); 697, Sep 2014; 520, Oct 2015; 530, Oct 2016. But numbers have since fallen again, with no annual peak since 2016 exceeding 300.

Pink-footed Goose   *Anser brachyrhynchus*

A very rare winter visitor.

It is possible (but not wholly likely) that feral birds may be involved, but some of the records occurred at times suggesting wild birds might have been involved. Five records.

1962	Jan 14th, 1 (injured)
1982 Ivy Lake	Feb 23rd
2008 Ibsley Water	Dec 8th
2010 Ibsley Water	intermittently Sep 26th-Oct 25th
2017 Ibsley Water	1cy, Nov 1st-end of year (probably died); ad, Dec 24th-Jan 25th 2018

Tundra Bean Goose   *Anser serrirostris*

A very rare winter visitor from NE Europe/Siberia.

Two records. Both refer to the Russian-breeding form *rossicus*, now treated as a subspecies of the newly-split 'Tundra Bean Goose', which is much the commoner of the two Bean Geese to occur in southern England.

2005	Jan 30th (2 flew in to Ibsley water-meadows from the SE, and thus presumably over the Lakes
2008 Ibsley Water	Dec 14th-Jan 26th 2009 (roosted regularly)

White-fronted Goose   **Anser albifrons**

Once a regular visitor, but now a very rare winter visitor.

Prior to the mid-1990s, when this species wintered in some numbers in the Avon Valley, many White-fronted Geese used Ibsley Water (especially) as a night-time roost (e.g. 360, Dec 14th 1981). With the near total demise of that flock, records have recently become irregular and infrequent, and with very few birds involved.

All records since 1996 are given below.

1996 Ibsley Water	66 roosted, Jan 28th; 29 roosted, Dec 30th
1997 Ibsley Water	37 Feb 9th; 3 Dec 13th; 2-3 Dec 26th-27th
2004 Spinnaker Lake	Jan 23rd
2004 Ibsley Water	12 (8 ad + 4 1cys) Dec 24th
2009 Ibsley Water	2cy roosted regularly Feb 8th-Mar 8th; also Apr 4th
2010 Ibsley Water	11 roosted regularly Feb 7th-17th; 1 ad until Mar 13th; 5, Dec 8th-17th, 1 1cy staying until 2011

2011 Ibsley Water   11 regular during Jan, until Feb 2nd

2016 Ibsley Water   1cy, Dec 10th-11th

2017 Ibsley Water   2cy, intermittently Jan 13th-Mar 2nd 2018 (probably same)

Mute Swan   *Cygnus olor*

A common resident and passage migrant/winter visitor. Recent decline.

Some dozens of Mute Swans are nearly always present around the Lakes, and numbers increase both in late summer, with post-fledging dispersal, and again (but not always) in winter. Peak annual counts between 1996 and 2004 averaged approximately 93, but from 2009 an apparent change in status occurred, with a record count of 177 on July 11th 2009, 134 in both Oct and Nov the following year, and a sensational all-time record of 244 on July 31st 2011. This remarkable count has been followed by a steady and quite marked decline in more recent years, to an annual maximum as low as 58 in 2015. Numbers are back at or slightly below the levels seen around the millennium.

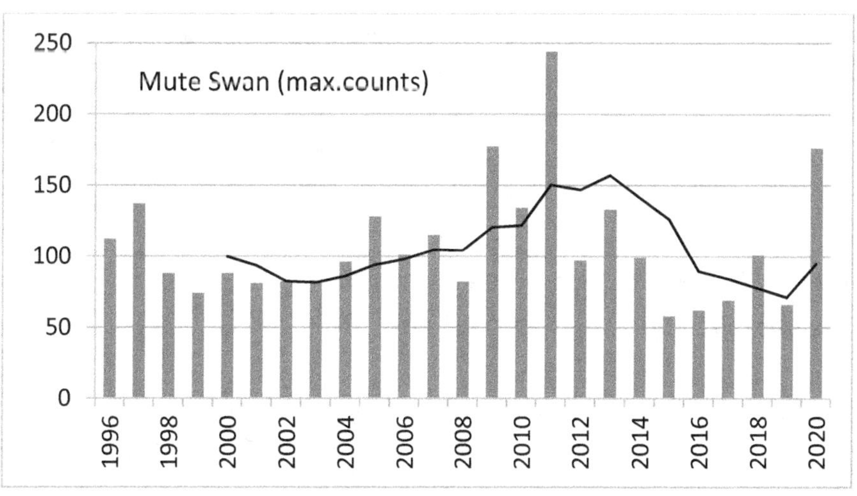

Bewick's Swan *Cygnus columbianus*

A scarce winter visitor, much reduced in recent years.

Until the 1990s, a sizeable herd of Bewick's Swans was a big feature of the Avon Valley in winter, with grounded flocks often feeding at Harbridge and elsewhere close to the Lakes. Indeed, large flocks regularly flew in to Blashford Lakes every evening in the winter to roost (e.g. 156, Ivy Lake, Jan 25th 1981, 113, Jan 18th 1982). However, in recent years, the numbers have dwindled almost to vanishing point. In 1993 it was noted in *HBR* that there was no regular roosting, and in 1995 none whatsoever spent the night at Ibsley Water for the first time in many years. 1996 and 1997 saw a return to better numbers, with up to 81 and 69 roosting at each end of the years, but the 21st century saw further decline.

2001 saw just two records of 14 individuals, and then there were no more firmly recorded as being on the Lakes until three records of nine birds in total in late 2008. 2009-11 each saw up to 20 birds each, but only on two or three dates. Up to six roosted regularly on Ibsley Water in early 2012, but only one was recorded (once) in late 2012. The species now has to be classed as a rare winter visitor, and it remains to be seen whether the flocks of yesteryear ever return. Records in full since 2013:

2013 Ibsley Water	Mar 3rd,9th,10th; Dec 29th
2014 Ibsley Water	Jan 28th, Nov 28th-29th
2015 Ibsley Water	2, Mar 10th
2016 Ibsley Water	Jan 18th; Dec 28th
2018 Ibsley Water	ad, Feb 5th

In 1987, a Whistling Swan (*C. c. columbianus*, the nominate Nearctic form) was present for much of Jan in the Avon Valley. Whether it was ever recorded at Blashford Lakes is at present unclear.

Whooper Swan   *Cygnus cygnus*
A very rare winter visitor.

The specifics of two recent records, but possibly some from earlier years, when the species was more regular in the Avon Valley, have been lost. The species has become rather more frequent in Hampshire in recent years, and more records might be expected.

1988 Mockbeggar Lake	Dec 30th
2008 Rockford Lake	3 ads, Nov 23rd

Egyptian Goose   *Alopochen aegyptiaca*
Until recently, a rare visitor, but now a breeding resident.

All records refer to birds deriving from the rapidly expanding feral populations, until recently centred on NE Hants.

1993 Ibsley Water	Apr 25th-July 29th;
	3, Aug 26th
1993 Snails Lake	Oct 3rd
1996 Ibsley Water	2, July 28th, Aug 24th and 31st
1998 Ibsley Water	pair, June 19th-20th, then 3 until Aug 2nd;
	later 2 on Oct 3rd
1999 Ibsley Water	pair, June 26th-Aug 8th
2000 Ibsley Water	2, July 16th and 22nd
2001	July 15th
2002	June 20th-July 14th
2004	1-2, Jan 11th-Apr 12th; 3, Aug 6th
2005	Jun 9th and July 3rd;
	3 from Aug 21st-Sep 1st
2006	2-3, July 10th-Aug 6th
2007	7, Sep 30th

    Apr 15th; 4, Aug 1st-Oct 26th; 4, Nov 7th; 5, Nov 16th-20th

From 2009 onwards, records became too frequent for full details to be kept. In that year a maximum of nine was recorded in Aug. In 2010, a pair with 6 young was seen on Rockford Lake on Aug 14th, but they were suspected of not having been hatched locally. In 2011, breeding finally occurred, at Rockford Lake, with three young raised, and up to 21 were present in late summer. Seven young were hatched in 2012, including an extraordinarily pale (likely leucistic) individual, christened "Rameses".

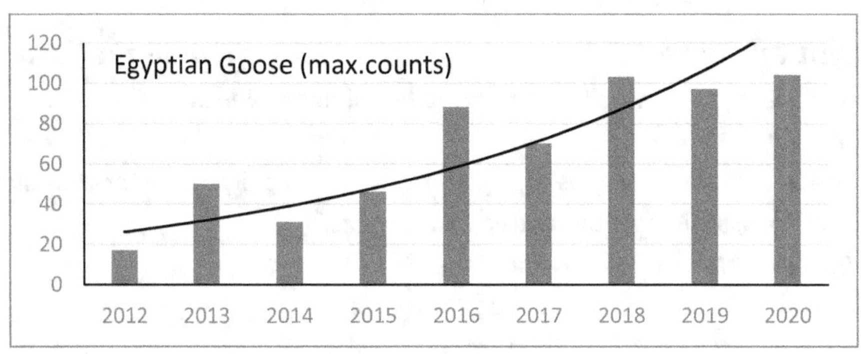

In the past decade, numbers have only grown and grown. The site peak is 104 in 2018, but the species is now so familiar that counts are irregular and that figure is likely an underestimate. See comments under Shelduck below regarding the possible ecological impact of this invasive alien species.

Shelduck   *Tadorna tadorna*

Regularly present in small numbers, with breeding usually occurring. Has declined in recent years.

The all-time record stands at 55, recorded on May 22nd 1993, reflecting the usual peak in spring, between Mar and May. Since 2005, annual maximum counts have averaged 15, but since 2009, maxima have been just 8, 10 and 9, compared with 24 as recently as Feb 2007. Just 24 and 26 "bird months" were recorded in 2010 and 2011 respectively. This number declined to 18 and 15 in 2015 and 2016 respectively. The peak in (Feb) 2020 is probably misleading, as it included adjacent areas of the Avon Valley.

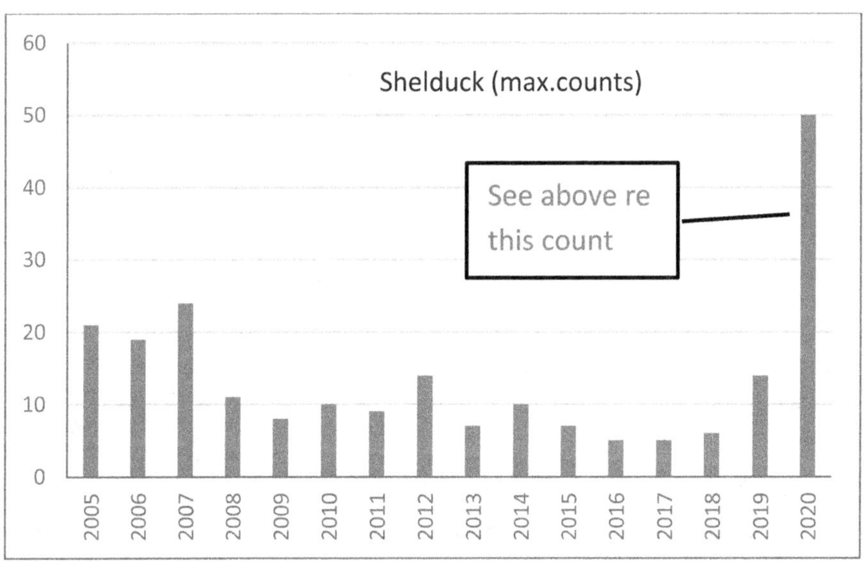

Up to two pairs have been recorded breeding in most years. However, the decline of the Shelduck at Blashford is more than likely connected to the meteoric rise of the Egyptian Goose. The latter species may occupy holes suitable for Shelduck, or indeed oust occupiers.

Mandarin Duck   *Aix galericulata*

A scarce resident and breeder.

The status of Mandarins at Blashford was formerly shrouded in mystery. They evidently used to be quite regular visitors from their breeding grounds in the New Forest and perhaps elsewhere, but they became much harder to see at the Lakes for many years, for reasons unknown. Very recently, they have increased once more, and regularly breed. There are huge gaps in the data, such that the date of the first record is unknown, and the highest count can only be an educated guess! The records which follow should be treated as selected highlights over the years, and are *deliberately incomplete.*

1981	first recorded – no dates on record
1995	first since 1981; 2, Jan 10th; 4, June 4th and 10th; 1-7, Oct 17th-Dec 29th
2000	only two records 52 (all-time record), Aug 30th; 6, Sep 24th
2001	noted in five months; max 23 in Aug

Annual from 2001 onwards bar 2005 and 2009, but often only one or two records per year

2014 Mockbeggar Lake	5 broods
2015 Mockbeggar Lake	4 broods
2017	max 69, Oct

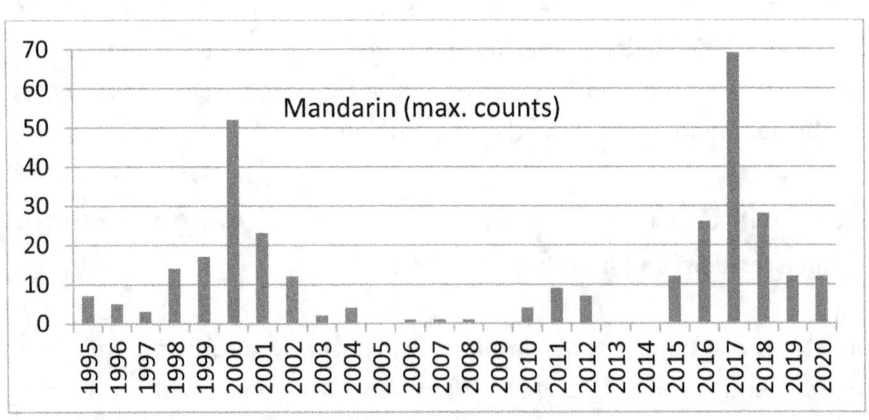

Garganey   *Spatula querquedula*

A rare passage migrant.

50 records of some 90 birds.

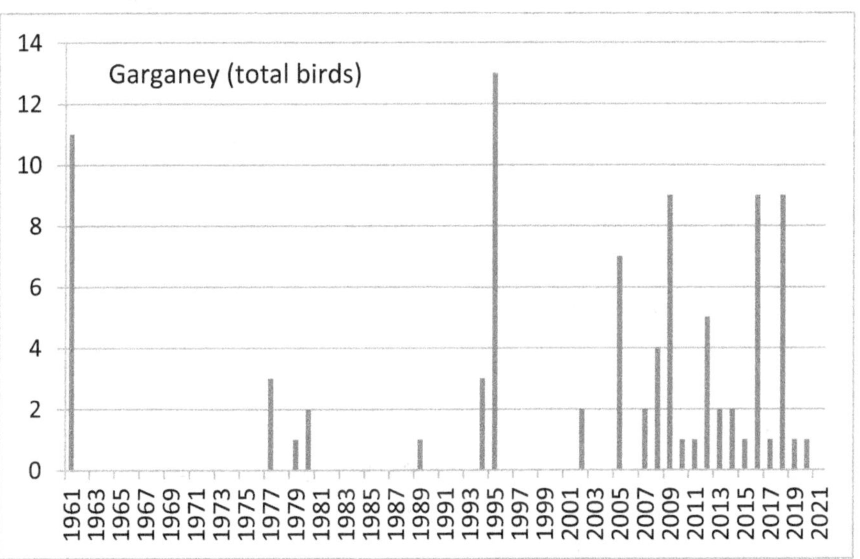

As the graph indicates, there are occasional "big" years, but the overall trend is towards more regular occurrence in recent years, probably because of better coverage. 57% have been in spring (between Mar 22nd and May 19th) and 42% in autumn (between Aug 14th and Oct 20th). The overall mean occurrence rate is 1.5 per year, but in years when Garganeys *are* recorded, the mean is 4.1, indicating both influx years and multiple occurrences such as the remarkable (up to) 11 in Mar and May 1961, seven in late Aug 1995, and seven on Apr 6th 2018.

On two occasions, records have indicated possible breeding. In 1996, a pair was present on Jun 16th, and an eclipse drake on Sep 15th. In 2008, two males were present on Mar 23rd, with further (or one of the same) drakes seen May 3rd and 19th, and another sighting in high summer on July 6th. No females (let alone ducklings) have ever been seen in summer, but Garganeys are highly secretive breeders and often go undetected.

Shoveler   *Spatula clypeata*
A common winter visitor, with an increase in recent years.

Shovelers form a conspicuous and sometimes very numerous part of the dabbling duck community at Blashford Lakes in winter, and the population size is of often of National, and very rarely **International Importance**. Peak numbers are generally found early in the new year, and, as with other ducks, fluctuate with valley and weather conditions.

A triple figure count was not made until 1977 (145 in Dec), and an extraordinary 430 were standing on a frozen Spinnaker Lake on Feb 12th 1978, but after a peak of 238 in Dec 1996, the species seemed to be in the doldrums. In 2003, numbers bounced back up spectacularly, reaching 428 in Feb (surpassing the then **International Importance** threshold), and peak counts have averaged over 200 since then.

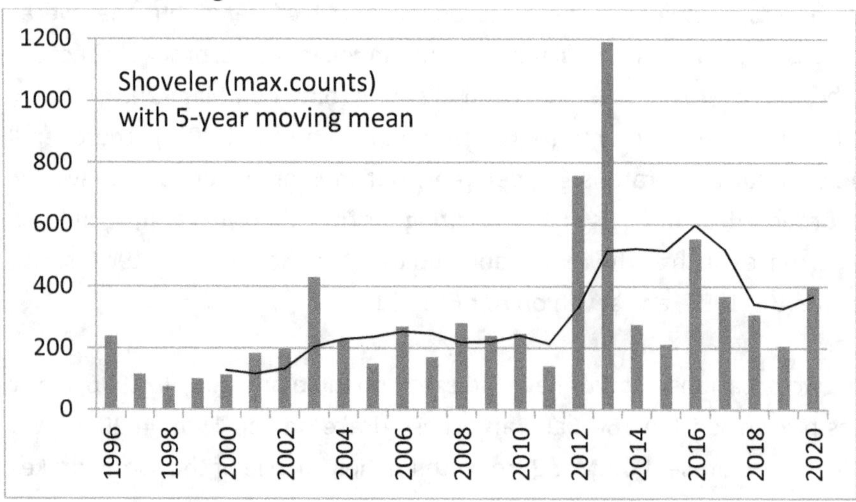

However, events of 2012-13 eclipsed all this. 757 were counted feeding on a major algal bloom at Ibsley Water in Dec 2012, and numbers continued to grow, to an astonishing 1190 in Jan 2013. This is equivalent to 183% of the current **International Importance** threshold. Almost 3% of all north-west Europe's Shovelers were on one lake at Blashford at that time.

Gadwall   *Mareca strepera*

A common winter visitor and scarce breeder – increased in recent years.

Until the early 1980s, Gadwall were rare in Hampshire. Singles were recorded at Blashford Lakes in 1970 and 1975, and 23 were seen in 1976, including a (then) exceptional 18 on Dec 27th. In 1983, the year breeding was first confirmed in Hampshire, 116 were counted at Blashford Lakes in Oct. An explosive increase then occurred, with considerable inter-annual fluctuations. Peak numbers are generally present around the turn of the year, and rise significantly in colder weather. 1017 were counted in Jan 2008, and this was in turn eclipsed by 1149 on Jan 16th 2011, and 1197 on Dec 16th 2012. Numbers have been lower in more recent winters, back at the levels seen around the millennium. The 2020 peak of just 427 was lower than any since 1989. Breeding was first recorded in 1997 (3 pairs), and up to six broods have been seen annually since then.

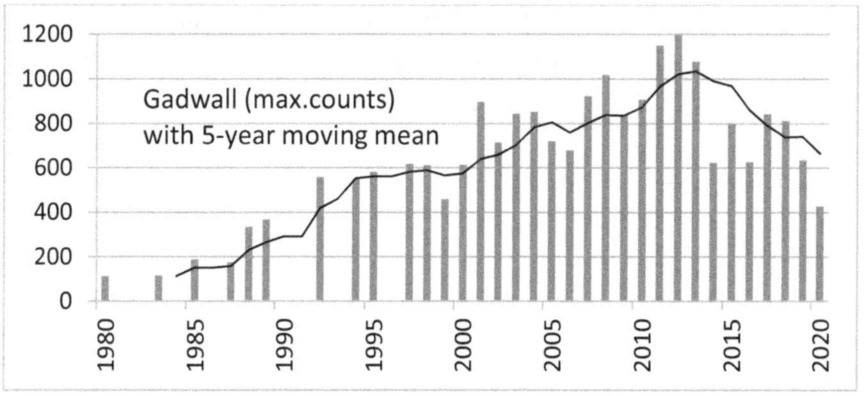

Blashford Lakes (and the surrounding Avon Valley) are a site of **National Importance** for Gadwall. Only Rutland Water and the Ouse Washes hold more in winter, and at its peak in 2012, the Blashford birds comprised an astonishing 5.7% of the entire British wintering population. Gadwall, being surface feeders, are largely dependent on Coot bringing clumps of waterweed up from the depths of their favoured lakes, and can often be seen associating closely with that species.

Wigeon   *Mareca penelope*
A common winter visitor. A few generally oversummer.

Large numbers of Wigeon use the Avon valley in winter, and many of them roost or loaf at Blashford Lakes. The numbers occurring each winter vary quite widely, in response to flood levels in the valley and weather conditions.

Complete data for Blashford Lakes alone (i.e. not including counts from the valley) are available only since 1996. During the period since then, maximum numbers have ranged from just 728, right up to 2795, on Dec 30th 1996. The largest counts invariably occur when shooting in the valley moves almost all the local wildfowl onto the Lakes. The median maximum count since 1996 has been 1456. There does appear to have been a real decline since 2015. This may be due to milder winters or changes in habitat suitability. Very small numbers often oversummer.

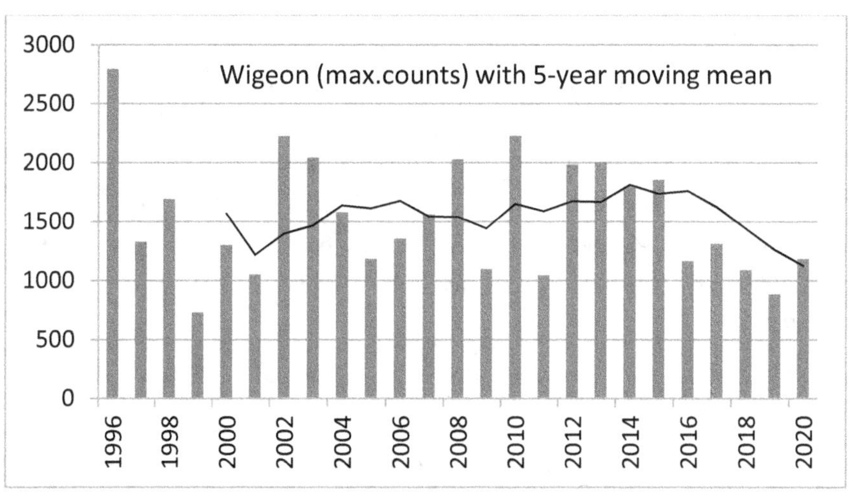

American Wigeon   *Mareca americana*
A very rare winter visitor from North America.

One record.

1984 Ivy Lake   ♂, Feb 12th-19th

[2008 Ibsley Water   probable ♀ reported, Dec 19th]

We are perhaps due another, given the relative frequency of this species in southern Britain, and the sometimes large numbers of Eurasian Wigeon which use the Lakes.

Mallard   *Anas platyrhynchos*
A common resident and winter visitor, but declining.

Reasonable numbers of Mallard are generally present year round at the Lakes, and several broods are found annually, although success is generally low. One female nested in a witches' broom on a birch tree in 2010, some six metres off the ground! A substantial winter influx occurs each year, but as with other wildfowl, the numbers involved vary considerably.

In recent years, a significant and steady decline appears to have taken hold, a fact reflecting the county and regional trend. Since 1995, winter maximum counts have averaged 303, but only two maxima have exceeded that mean since 2007, and none since 2009. The highest count is of 561 in Nov 1997.

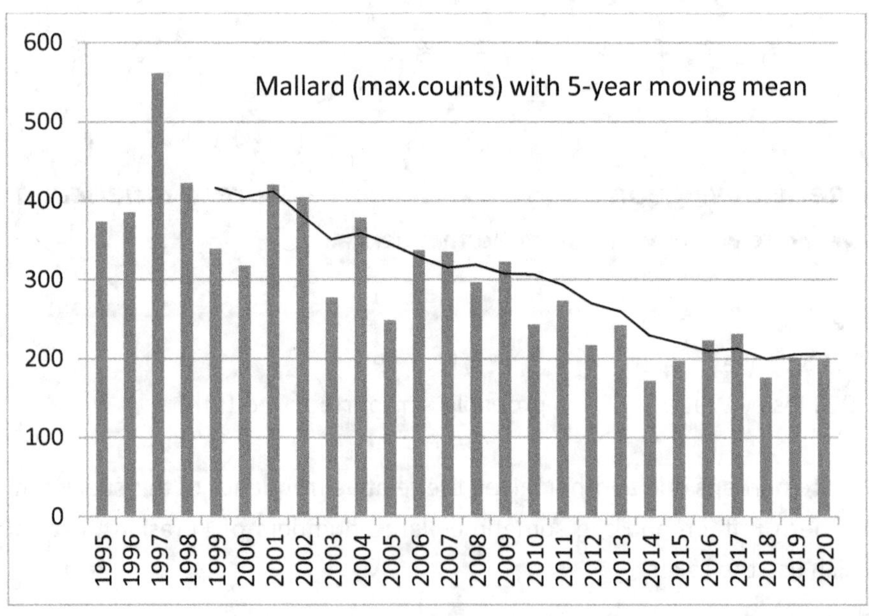

Pintail   *Anas acuta*

Formerly a scarce winter visitor, showing signs of an erratic increase, but now a generally common winter visitor with occasional major influxes.

Double figure winter counts were rare until the early 2000s, and the number of bird months was often below 30. The maximum count was just

42 in Jan 2001. All that changed in 2003, when a massive influx meant Blashford Lakes briefly qualified as a site of **National Importance**, with a remarkable 400 recorded in Feb. Normal service was quickly resumed in subsequent winters, but 2007 saw a further large arrival, with up to 215 in Feb, and maxima of 99 and 127 in the two following years. After this period, numbers declined once again, but it seems likely that the Lakes can look forward to occasional large influxes of this spectacular duck, as in the winters of 2012-14, and in early 2020, when the record was broken again with 545 on Jan 27th. Very occasionally, birds oversummer (e.g. in 2011).

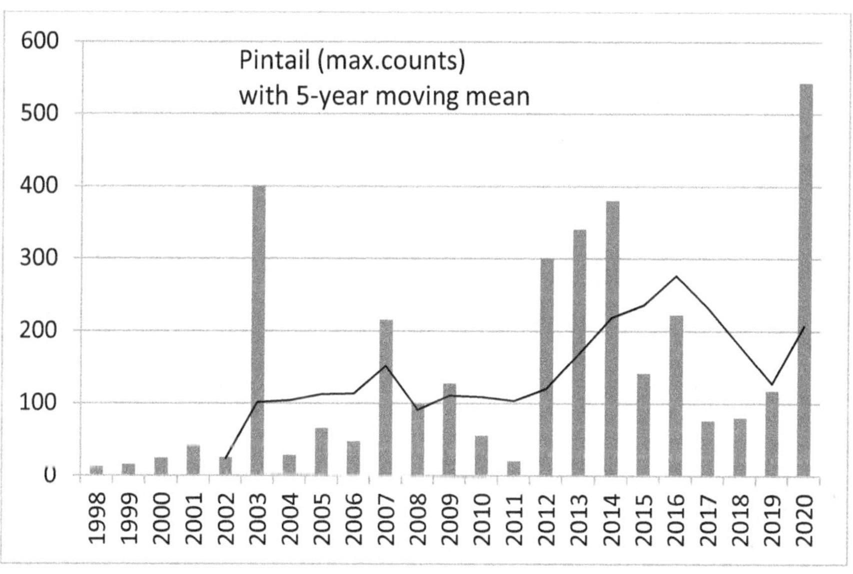

Teal   *Anas crecca*

A common winter visitor in varying numbers – small numbers summer.

The Avon Valley has long been an important site for Teal, and significant numbers use the Lakes both for feeding and for safe roosting. Maximum counts are generally in Dec/Jan. Numbers fluctuate significantly from year to year, but have generally been in the region of 250-500 in recent winters, with the exception of 2002/03 and 2012/13, when much higher numbers occurred. 1125 in Dec 2000 was the first four-figure count, and this was further exceeded by 1531 in Dec 2002, rising to 2292 in Feb 2003. The count reached 1637 in late 2012. In the last few years, numbers have returned to much lower levels.

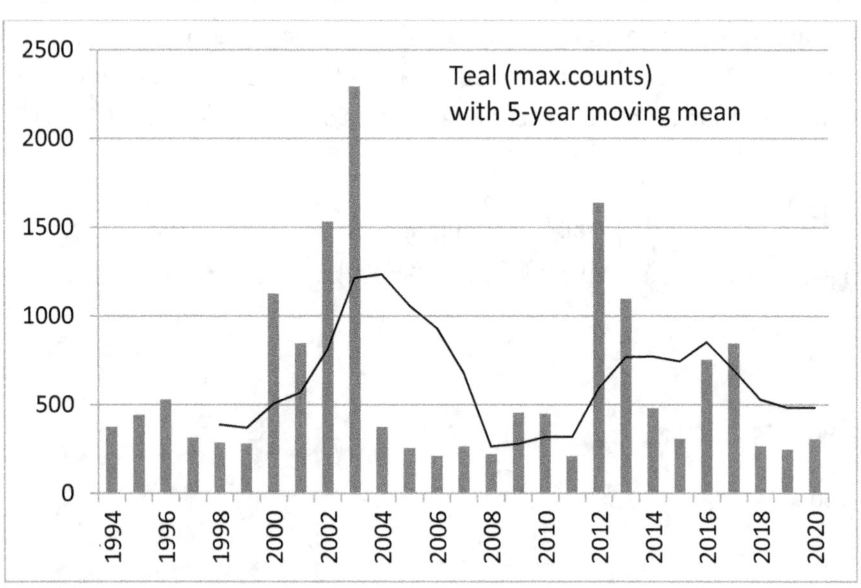

Green-winged Teal   *Anas carolinensis*
A very rare winter visitor from North America.

Three records of two birds.
1980 Ivy Lake   ♂, Jan 12th
2013 Ivy Lake   ♂, Jan 26th, Feb 6th-15th
2014 Ibsley Water   ♂, Apr 6th-8th (same)

The ten day (apparent) absence of the second bird, during which time the bird was being actively sought, suggests strongly that there is considerable turnover and relocation by this and other wildfowl species during the winter. Interchange with nearby water bodies, such as Longham Lakes, has strongly been suspected for certain rare species, notably Smew, which have a similar habit of "going missing" for lengthy periods. The 2017 Bonaparte's Gull and Lesser Scaup finally confirmed the theory!

Red-crested Pochard   *Netta rufina*
A rare winter visitor. All records likely from feral British populations.

24 records of 33-38 birds, all since Jan 11th 1985 (apart from an apparently released bird in 1980). Records became more regular and involved more birds in the early 21st century, in line with the growth of the feral population centred on the Cotswold Water Park in Wilts/Glos. The reason for the more recent drop-off in records may well be a lack of cold winter periods displacing birds from other regions.

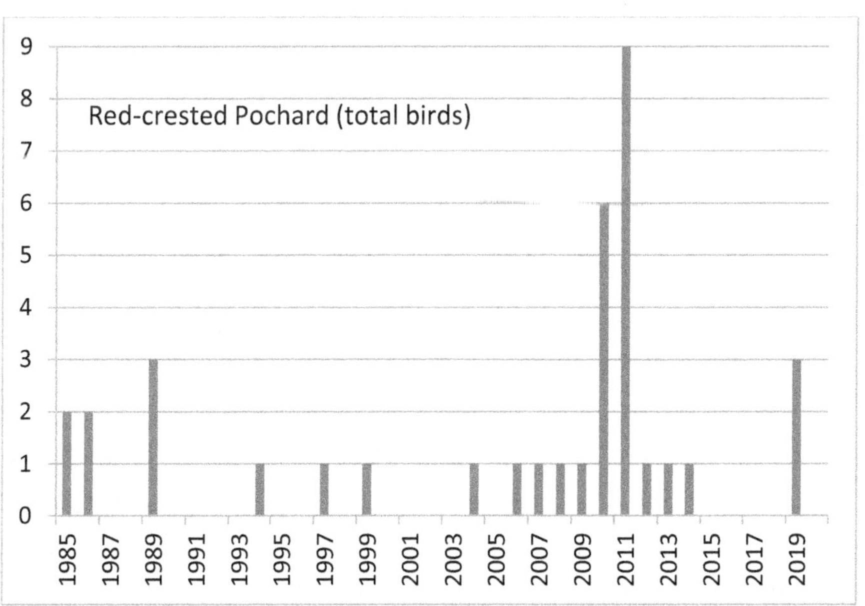

Pochard   *Aythya ferina*

A common winter visitor which occasionally oversummers and has bred. Has shown a recent, marked decline.

In the 1960s, scattered counts indicate up to 100 in winter at the Lakes. Much larger counts only began to be recorded about 1983, when 369 were counted in Dec. This was further eclipsed by 431 in Nov 1985, and a county record 655 on Nov 5th 1988. Numbers continued close to this high level for several subsequent winters, reaching 650 in Dec 1996 and the all-time high of 690 on Jan 18th 2003.

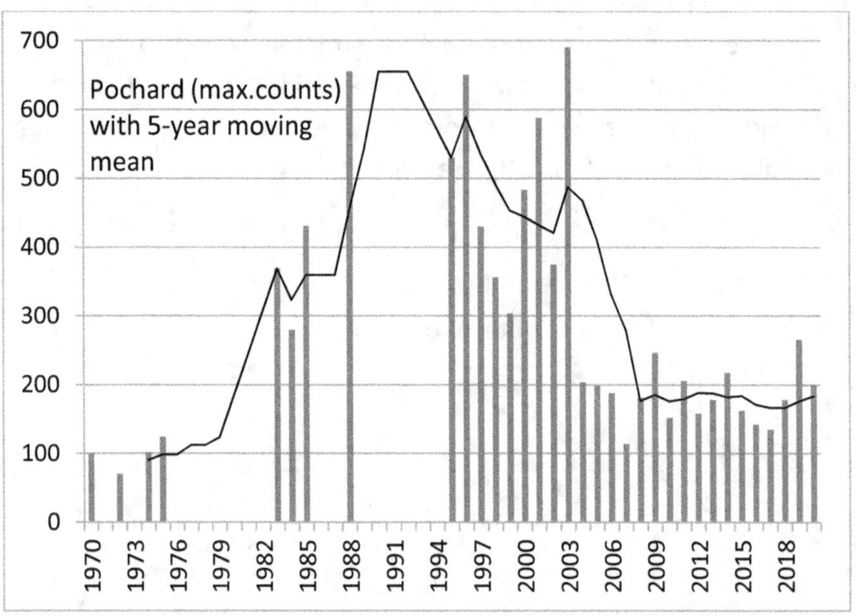

However, immediately after this peak, numbers more than halved, and maximum counts since 2004 have averaged only 183, with a peak of 246 in Feb 2009, and a "lowest annual high" of just 113 in 2007. It would appear that some combination of population decline further afield and perhaps a shift in wintering distribution/weather patterns is taking its toll on numbers of this duck.

A pair bred on Ellingham Lake in 1986, the first such record for the Avon Valley, and behaviour suggestive of breeding has been recorded occasionally since. A female with two ducklings was seen in July 2012, and three pairs were noted on May 20th 2014. A very few are present all summer every year.

Ferruginous Duck   *Aythya nyroca*

A very rare winter visitor from eastern Europe.

Two birds have been recorded, plus there is an old, unverified report.

[1973	pair, Jan 14th]
1987 Mockbeggar Lake	ad ♂, Dec 13th-16th
2011 Spinnaker Lake	Dec 30th-Jan 14th 2012
2012-early 2021	same, every winter, mostly on Kingfisher Lake

This species is a rare one indeed in Hampshire. Only about 12 birds are accepted as having occurred in the county since the first in 1960. It has become so rare that it was readmitted to the BBRC list of 'official' national rarities in 2017. The regular male of 2011 onwards is currently the most regularly occurring Ferruginous Duck in Britain.

Ring-necked Duck   *Aythya collaris*

A very rare winter visitor from North America.

Six records of (probably) five individuals. The 1991 and 1993 records refer to the regularly returning drake which frequented Timsbury Gravel Pits for many winters.

1979-81 Various lakes	ad ♂, Dec 15th-Feb 17th 1980; Dec 29th 1980-Jan 11th 1981.
1985 Spinnaker Lake	ad ♂, Jan 31st
1987 Mockbeggar Lake	1cy, Nov 16th-17th
1991 Linbrook Lake	ad ♂, Nov 16th-27th
1993	ad ♂, Mar 27th
2020 Ibsley Water	ad ♂, Apr 16th-17th

Tufted Duck   *Aythya fuligula*

A common winter visitor and occasional breeder.

Winter maxima of this species have averaged 488 since 2001. This figure is not too different from data stretching (fragmentarily) back some two decades before that. The all-time record count was of 705 on Nov 5th 1988, which is still a county record count. The maximum since has been 608 on Apr 6th 2014. As with other wildfowl, numbers vary from year to year, but have held up well in recent winters (cf. Pochard). Up to eight pairs have been known to breed at the Lakes in a single year, but breeding is not proved every year. In 2013, a remarkable 30 pairs bred at Ibsley North Lake; this fell to just five in 2014.

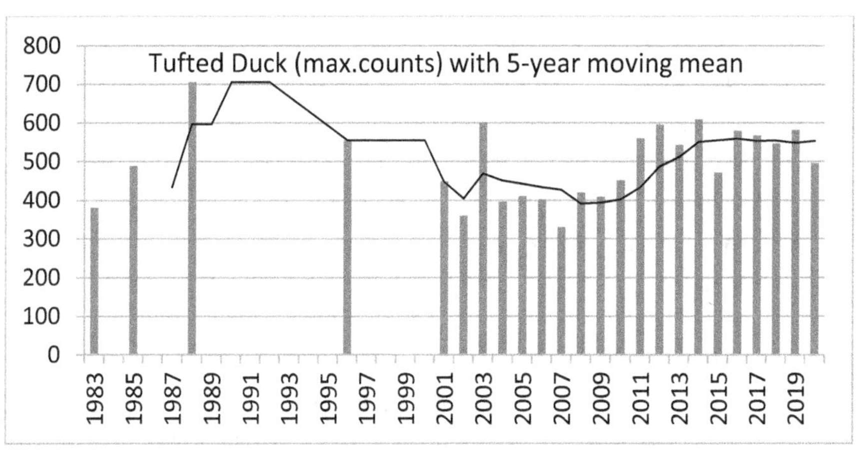

Scaup   *Aythya marila*

A rare passage migrant and winter visitor.

36 records involving about 44 individuals. It is possible that some of the older records refer to hybrid *Aythya* ducks. One such is square-bracketed below and not included in the totals.

1960	♂, Jan 5th
1969 Kingfisher Lake	2cy ♂, Jan 18th
1978 Ellingham Lake	Mar 5th-12th; Apr 27th-May 8th (presumed same)
1985	Nov 30th-Dec 31st; 2, Dec 15th
1986 Snails Lake	♀, Jan 1st-6th
1987	♀, Jan 18th-19th; Feb 28th-Mar 1st
1988 Mockbeggar Lake	ad ♂, Sep 18th
1989 Mockbeggar Lake	2 ♀ types, Jan 11th
1992	♀, Jan 12th-Apr 3rd; 2cy ♂ Apr 4th

1995 Mockbeggar Lake ♀, Jan 22nd-Feb 22nd

1996 Spinnaker Lake ♂, Dec 27th-30th, also Jan 1st 1997

1997 Mockbeggar Lake 3 (♂, ♀, 2cy ♂), Jan 26th

1998 Mockbeggar Lake ♂, Jan 17th; pair, Jan 18th

1998 Ivy Lake 1cy ♂, Dec 31st

2000 Mockbeggar Lake ♂, Jan 30th; ♀ Dec 29th

[2001 Snails Lake probable hybrid ♀/1cy, Dec 30th-Mar 3rd 2002]

2005 Ibsley Water ♀, Sep 18th

2010 Ibsley Water ♂, Apr 8th-17th; 1cy ♂, Oct 14th; ♀, Oct 31st

2011 ♀, Jan 15th; ♀, Mar 20th-26th

2011 Ibsley Water 1, Oct 8th; 2, Oct 9th

2012 Ibsley Water ♂, Mar 13th and 24th-25th; same, Apr 10th-13th

2015 Kingfisher Lake ♂, Jan 1st

2017 Ivy Lake 3, Jan 3rd (1 still on 11th)

2017 Ibsley Water Feb 19th; Mar 11th-25th

2019 various lakes 1cy, Oct 26th-Dec 4th

2020 Ibsley Water 2cy, Jan 1st

2021 Rockford Lake ♂, Feb 11th-Apr 18th (also on Ibsley Water)

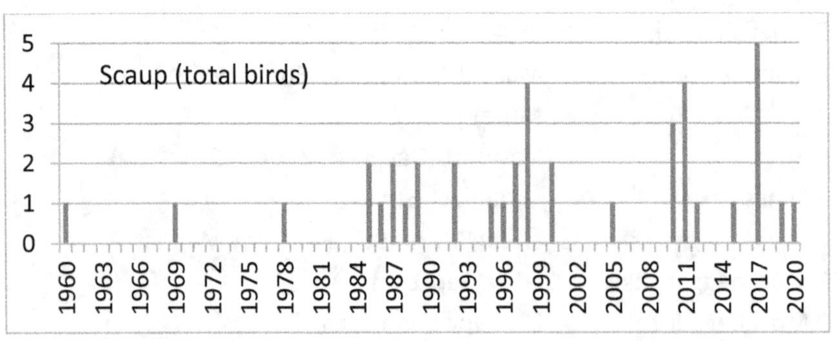

Lesser Scaup   *Aythya affinis*

A very rare vagrant.

One record.

2017 various lakes	ad ♂, Oct 28th-Nov 4th
2018 Ibsley Water	Feb 3rd-4th (same)
2019 Ibsley Water	Jan 20th (presumed same)

The long-awaited and long-predicted first for Hampshire and Blashford was found on Spinnaker Lake by Alan Lewis, conveniently on a Saturday morning. It had previously been seen at Longham Lakes in Dorset, and was being actively searched for once it had gone missing from that site! It was the 26th species of duck to have been recorded at Blashford. Despite it having been seen on Snails Lake on a couple of occasions, the author's best efforts with a ladder failed to get it on his garden list. Local fireworks displays appear to have scared it off in the end, but it returned in early 2018 and 2019.

Eider   *Somateria mollissima*

A very rare winter visitor.

One record.

2016 Ibsley Water	immature, Nov 22nd

A very remarkable but perhaps not wholly unexpected record – what *was* unexpected was that it arrived on the same day as four Pale-bellied Brent Geese, also new for the site!

Velvet Scoter   *Melanitta fusca*

A very rare passage migrant.

One record.
1985 Spinnaker Lake   Mar 9th

Another would be very welcome indeed!

Common Scoter   *Melanitta nigra*

A very rare visitor.

16 records of upwards of 25 birds. Quite regular in recent years, but mostly mercurial in its visits.

1995 Ibsley Water	♀, June 20th-22nd
2002 Ellingham Lake	pair, July 14th
2007 Rockford Lake	Sep 30th
2009 Ibsley Water	♀, July 18th
2010 Ibsley Water	♂, Feb 16th
2013 Ibsley Water	2♀♀, Dec 3rd
2014 Ibsley Water	♂, Mar 15th; ♂, Mar 25th
2015 Ibsley Water	♂, Oct 20th; ♀, Nov 21st
2016 Ibsley Water	♂, Mar 21st; ♀, June 23rd-July 5th; ♂, Sep 5th
2019 Ibsley Water	♀ type, Oct 29th
2020 Snails Lane	c.10 south at night, Oct 17th
2021 Ibsley Water	juv, July 20th

Four of the records have been in high summer, which is (perhaps surprisingly) not unusual in a southern English context. Annual records 2013-2016 and 2019-21 are notable.

Long-tailed Duck　　　　　　　　　*Clangula hyemalis*

A very rare winter visitor.

Twelve records, all but one of single birds. In contrast to the previous species, eight of the eleven birds were long-stayers.

1968	♂, Apr 13th
1970 Kingfisher Lake	♀, Nov 14th-24th
1981 various lakes	2 ♀♀, Nov 14th-Dec 12th
1982 Mockbeggar Lake	♀, Nov 26th-Mar 14th 1983
1991 Spinnaker Lake	Dec 24th-May 3rd 1992
1993	♀ Nov 21st- May 8th 1994
2008	♂, Nov 14th-25th
2010 Rockford Lake	1cy, Nov 15th-19th
2014 Ibsley Water	2cy ♂, May 4th; 1cy ♂ Nov 15th-Dec 31st
2015 (mostly) Ibsley Water	2cy ♂ Jan 1st-Mar 27th (same)
2019 Ibsley Water	1cy, Nov 4th-Apr 23rd 2020
2020 Rockford Lake	imm ♂, Feb 3rd (probably same)

Goldeneye　　　　　　　　　*Bucephala clangula*

A scarce but regular winter visitor and passage migrant.

The first record is of two females on Jan 4th 1958, but birds were evidently scarcely seen until the 1970s. By the late 1970s, a wintering population had become established. Blashford Lakes now holds more birds than Langstone Harbour, traditionally the prime Hampshire site for the species. There is a late winter/early spring peak, usually in Mar, presumably involving an unknown proportion of "turnover birds" heading back north to their breeding grounds. Numbers were especially high in the mid-1980s, but then fell away sharply, to be followed by a recovery since the millennium. There appears to have been a further slow decline since about 2013.

The record count is of 64 (only 9 ♂♂) on Mockbeggar (44) and Ellingham (20) Lakes on Mar 1st 1987. Neither of these lakes is now favoured by Goldeneye, which are almost always found on Ibsley Water and Rockford Lakes these days. Females have summered in 1984 (also a ♂ until June that year) and 1990 (2).

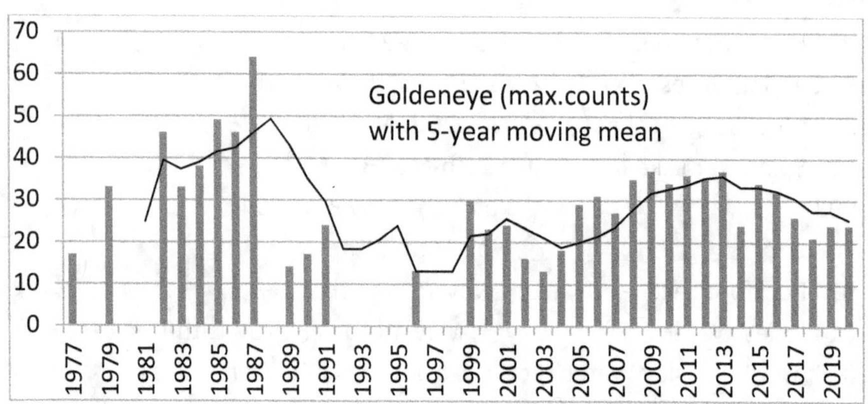

Smew   *Mergellus albellus*

A rare and irregular winter visitor from NE Europe.

Approximately 87 birds have been recorded, mostly since the mid-1980s. The first record was of a redhead on Feb 6th-14th 1960. The maximum counts were 10 in Jan-Feb 1985 and 9-12 in Jan-Feb 1997. Records are very patchily distributed, with significant peaks (perhaps involving returning birds) in the mid-1980s and the late 1990s.

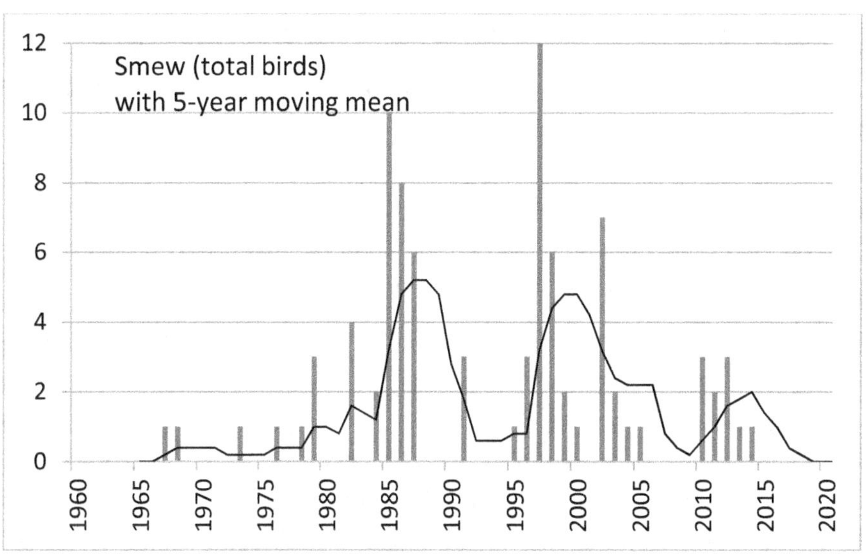

Smew have become very rare in recent winters across southern England, a pattern reflected at Blashford. All records since 2010 follow:

2009-10	redhead, over winter until Mar 13th
2010-11	redhead, Dec 12th-Mar 14th; 1cy ♂, Mar 16th-17th
2011-12	redhead, Dec 18th-Feb 28th; another, Feb 18th-25th; ad ♂, Feb 18th
2012-13	redhead, Dec 21st-Mar 30th
2013-14	redhead, Dec 5th-Feb 8th
2014-20	NO RECORDS
2021	2cy♂, Mockbeggar Lake, Feb 14th-22nd

Goosander   *Mergus merganser*

Formerly a rare winter visitor, now common, with a substantial roost gathering. Breeds nearby.

Until 1996, Goosanders were rare at Blashford Lakes. The first record was of a female on Jan 18th 1970, and only nine more were recorded (1971 and 1982 (8)) until 1983. Multiple records followed from 1985, when 11 were present in Jan, 3 were on Mockbeggar Lake and 11 flew over Spinnaker Lake in Feb, and a redhead was seen twice in Nov.

Subsequently, totals grew, but occurrences remained occasional and patchy, with 9 birds in 1986, 17 in 1987, no more until 1991 (1 bird), and then annual records since 1993. Double-figure maximum counts have been recorded since 1996, and have grown explosively since 2005, when a then remarkable 60 were present on Mar 6th. This upturn coincided with both a general increase in southern England, and the establishment of a small number of breeding pairs in the Avon Valley. Maximum counts are generally made at dusk when birds which have been feeding elsewhere (e.g. the River Avon and various New Forest ponds) come in to roost, but generally a few are present all day on Ibsley Water. Other lakes hold far fewer, but Goosanders are regularly seen on Snails, Spinnaker and Rockford Lakes, and less frequently on Ivy Lake.

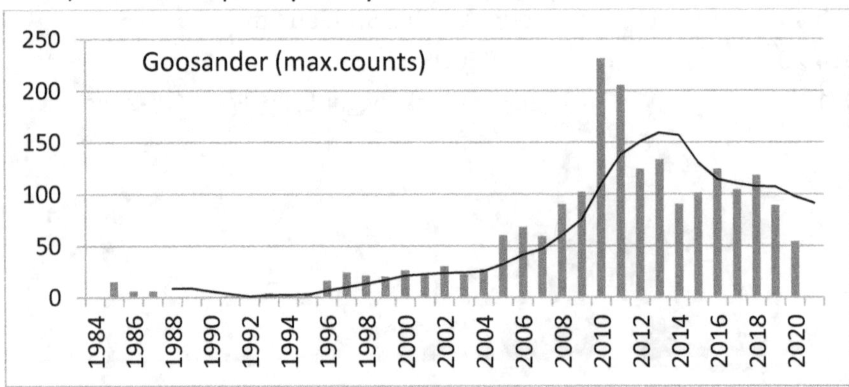

A further pulse of population growth occurred from 2008, when 90 were noted as present in Dec. Subsequent winter highs skyrocketed, with data for 2009-11 peaking at 102, 231 (record count, 31st Dec 2010) and 205 respectively. 2012 counts were lower (max. 85, Feb 10th) and that trend has continued, with roost totals since typically peaking at around 100, but much lower in 2019 and 2020. More birds stay for longer periods of the year, too, with occasional summer records now frequent. Goosanders are now established as a popular and regular part of the birding scene at Blashford.

Red-breasted Merganser *Mergus serrator*
A very rare winter visitor.

15 records of 21-23 birds.

1971	3, Mar 26th; pair, Dec 18th
1979 Spinnaker Lake	redhead, Feb 18th
1980 Ellingham Lake	redhead, Nov 16th
1984 Mockbeggar Lake	♂, Dec 8th
1990 Linbrook Lake	♂, Dec 9th
1996 Rockford Lake	redhead, Jan 16th
1996 Spinnaker Lake	redhead Feb 2nd (possibly same)
1996 Mockbeggar Lake	redhead, Dec 27th
1999	redhead, Jan 1st; pair, Jan 11th-24th
2010 Ibsley Water	3 roosted, Nov 7th, one of the same intermittently until Dec 31st
2011 Ibsley Water	♀, Jan 2nd-Mar 23rd
2012 Ibsley Water	redhead Jan 12th-Feb 25th (2, 25th), intermittently; redhead, Nov 15th (possibly a returning bird)
2014 Ibsley Water	2♂♂, Nov 21st

Ruddy Duck   *Oxyura jamaicensis*

**A formerly uncommon feral resident and breeder, now almost
extirpated nationally.**

The first Ruddy Duck for Blashford Lakes was not seen until 1981, when a
female/immature was on Ivy and Spinnaker Lakes from Nov 29th-Dec 19th.
Four were present in Jan and Feb 1982. A pair, and an extra male, were
present throughout the summer of 1985, and five young were raised. Five
were last seen on Nov 26th. Thereafter, Ruddy Ducks bred at Blashford
every year until at least 2005, with a maximum of three confirmed broods
in 1996.

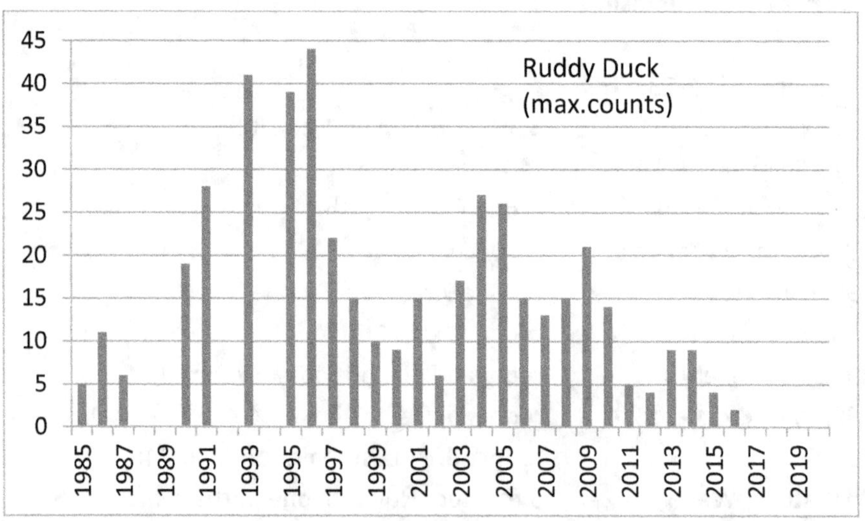

Oddly, maximum numbers peaked in the mid-1990s, with 44 on Mar 3rd
1996, but then declined quite steeply, even before the DEFRA-sponsored
eradication programme, which commenced in Sep 2006. Nationally,
numbers peaked in about 2000, when some 6,000 Ruddy Ducks were at
large. In 2005, a maximum of 135 bird-months was noted at Blashford.
Numbers held up well even after eradication began, with post-cull maxima

58

from 2006-2010 of 15, 13, 15, 21 and 14. Culls were performed at least twice at Blashford in 2010, and the 2011 maximum was of 5 on Feb 3rd, which was followed by a targeted cull of these birds. One was present in early 2012, until Feb 10th, and another was on Ibsley Water Nov 22nd. Surprisingly, up to 12 were noted scattered through 2013 (including a first-winter male in Dec), and 10 through 2014. There were two records of four birds in total in 2015, and two singles in 2016, the last on Ibsley Water on Sep 9th. None was seen in 2017 for the first time in 37 years, and none has been recorded since.

SMALLER WATERBIRDS SUMMARY

Provided as a summary, the graph below makes three things apparent:

1) There was a massive growth in wildfowl numbers from the 1980s
   to the millennium
2) There are very significant interannual variations (and n.b. the
   impact of the 2012/13 Shoveler plague, the 2011/12/13 Gadwall
   infestation, the 2003 and 2020 Pintail outbreaks and the 2002/03
   Teal glut
3) **Totals** numbers appear to be in decline – possible causes include
   climate change and habitat succession.

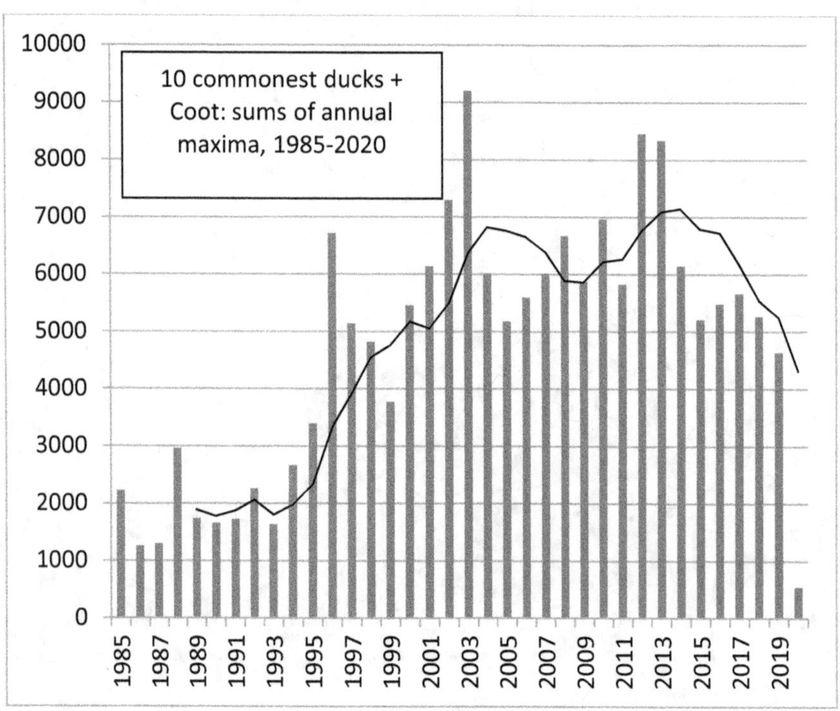

Pheasant   *Phasianus colchicus*

A frequent visitor, in small numbers.

Generally recorded at the Woodland Hide feeding station, and occasionally elsewhere.

Red-legged Partridge   *Alectoris rufa*

A very rare visitor.

This is a common and widespread species in the area (albeit not in the New Forest or Avon Valley as such), but the species is now vanishingly rare at the site, with only seven records since the turn of the millennium. There are quite plentiful records for the period 1995-99, with a maximum of 12 on Dec 8th 1996, when the species was described as "regular" on the new workings. One was at Ivy Lake on Apr 15th 2014, a typical date in the season when hormone-fuelled rogue males seem to wander into all kinds of strange habitats. The following year, one was at Ibsley Water just two days earlier (Apr 13th), with two the next day. One was at Ibsley Water by Goosander Hide on Jan 19th 2018.

Nightjar   *Caprimulgus europaeus*

A very rare summer visitor.

Six dated records of seven birds, four in the vicinity of Snails Lane.

1980	♂, June 11th
2011 Snails Lane	July 26th
2012 Snails Lane	May 17th
2014 Snails Lane	July 8th
2021 Ibsley Water	May 3rd
2021 North Poulner Lake	2, Sep 3rd

Nightjars do quite regularly wander down into the Avon Valley from nearby New Forest breeding sites, and have been noted on numerous occasions by ringers at pre-dawn and post-dusk trapping sessions. The above are, as suspected, a mere sample of records.

Swift   *Apus apus*
A common summer visitor and passage migrant.

Large numbers of Swifts feed in the airspace over the Lakes in spring and early summer. Several hundred are frequently present – e.g. 600, May 15th 2007; 400, June 4th 2012; 1000, June 5th-8th 2017; 1000, Apr 29th 2020.

Cuckoo   *Cuculus canorus*
A scarce passage migrant and summer visitor.

Cuckoos are heard and seen each spring, and presumably occasionally parasitize Reed Warblers and Dunnocks, but there is only one firm record of breeding (2020. A juvenile was picked up dead in Snails Lane in July 2021, but there is no evidence it was reared locally. Hepatic phase birds have been recorded at least twice.

Rock Dove/Feral Pigeon   *Columba livia*
A frequent visitor.

Feral Pigeons and domesticated racing pigeons are frequently recorded on and around the site.

Stock Dove   *Columba oenas*
A scarce visitor and breeder.

It would appear that Stock Doves are genuinely scarce at the site. They are occasionally seen at Ibsley Water, usually in flight, but there was (for instance) only one record during 2010-18 from a regularly watched Snails Lane garden. However, a (very tame) territorial pair took up residence in Snails Lane in early 2021, and bred in tall polar trees subsequently. 58 flew north over Ibsley Water in 40 minutes on Apr 16th 2017, but no autumn movements have been detected.

Woodpigeon   *Columba palumbus*
A common resident and passage migrant.

Woodpigeons are common and frequently seen around the area, with numbers rising in autumn and winter. In 2010, a substantial westwards movement, of several thousand birds, was noted on Nov 16th. Judging by reports of similar movements elsewhere in the region, such a passage probably occurs unobserved every year.

Turtle Dove   *Streptopelia turtur*

**A former summer visitor, now locally extirpated as a breeder, and very
rare on passage.**

1999	June 3rd
2008	May 19th
2010	one reported – no date
2015	2 flew west, Apr 18th

Seemingly on the brink of extirpation as a Hampshire bird, Turtle Doves
presumably once bred close to or in the area treated. The only hope for
records these days is of a very occasional passage migrant. The records
above are the only recent ones.

Collared Dove   *Streptopelia decaocto*

A common resident.

Frequent and sometimes abundant, but possibly recently declining. 91 at
North Poulner Lake on Jan 2nd 2018 appears to be the record count, but
now rare even at that regular pre-roost site.

Water Rail   *Rallus aquaticus*

An uncommon winter visitor and likely breeder.

Several are regularly present, but usually only seen from Ivy North Hide,
during the winter months. Seven were heard on Nov 30th 2014. Regular
spring/summer records suggest breeding occurs annually, and young have
been seen on more than one occasion.

Moorhen   *Gallinula chloropus*

A fairly common resident.

Large numbers are not a feature of Blashford Lakes, and the highest recorded count is of 39 in Oct 2014. Moorhens are present on most of the water bodies in small numbers, and a few pairs breed.

Coot   *Fulica atra*

A common resident, with larger numbers in winter.

Many pairs breed each year, but the extraordinary estimate of 80+ pairs in 1986 has not been approached in recent years. However, Blashford Lakes has at times been a site of **National Importance** for this species in winter, holding over 1% of the entire British population. 526 (a flock recorded in *HBR* as "massive") were counted in Nov 1982, but detailed data exist only since late 1985, since when the population roughly doubled, but has shown a more recent decline, with the 2020 peak the lowest ever recorded.

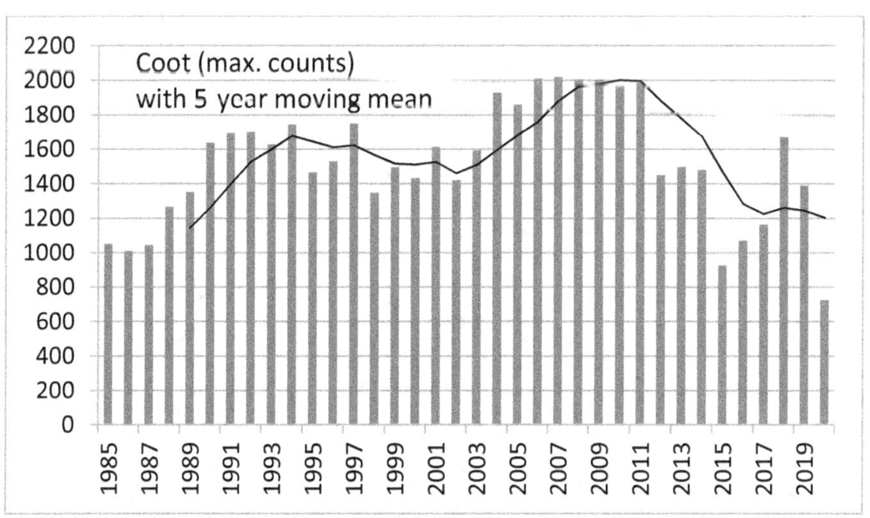

Much of the increase occurred in the early 1990s, and the population then stabilised at around the 2000 mark from about 2004, which is remarkably consistent, given that the all-time record is of 2019 on Dec 23rd 2007! Numbers have dropped back since 2012, by about 50% - the max. count failed to reach even 1000 in 2015, and was even lower in 2020. The peak counts are generally made in Nov or Dec, and tend to be higher during cold weather. Occasional migrants are heard at night in season.

Little Grebe   *Tachybaptus ruficollis*
A resident breeder and passage migrant/winter visitor.

This species exhibits autumn and (usually smaller) spring peaks, but birds are present year-round. Numbers have been broadly stable since at least 1992, with perhaps a slight increase after 2000, and a recent decline. The long-time maximum, a count of 72 on Aug 16th 1985, was finally bettered by 75 in Sep 2005, a count equalled in Oct just four years later. 80 in Aug 2013 was a new record. There are periods of dearth, often associated with freezing weather, as in winter 2010/11, when both Little and Great Crested Grebes almost completely vacated Blashford Lakes for the coast. Between six and 23 pairs have bred in recent years, averaging 13 a year, with varying success.

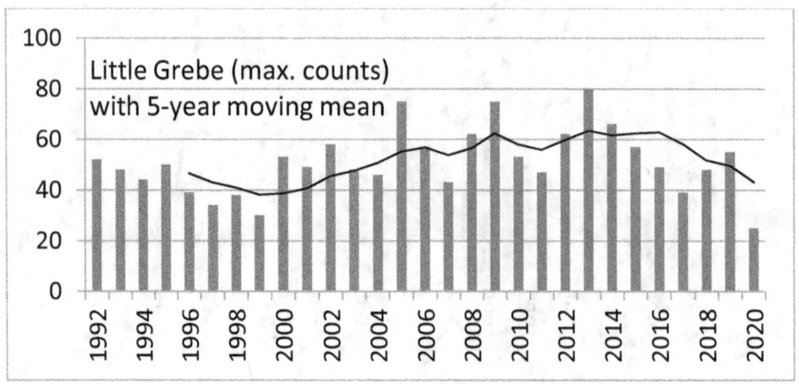

Red-necked Grebe　　　　　　　*Podiceps grisegena*

A very rare winter visitor.

Two records.

pre-1992 Ellingham Lake　　　date unknown
2007 Kingfisher Lake　　　　　Dec 28th

Red-necked Grebes are generally regarded as rather prone to inland occurrences in cold weather. While another is surely overdue, numbers have decreased in southern Britain in recent years. Any details of the first record above would be very welcome.

Great Crested Grebe　　　　　*Podiceps cristatus*

A resident breeder and common migrant/winter visitor.

Winter maxima prior to 1992 averaged about 35, with a peak count of 57 in Feb 1984. Since 1992, the species has become more common (with the pre-1992 record eclipsed in at least 75 months). Numbers are notably higher in late summer and autumn than they were, but still fall perplexingly low at times. The years since about 2007 have seen lower counts in winter, despite some high autumn maxima. The peak count is now most commonly in Sep. The record count is of 128 in Sep 2018.

Breeding has occurred since at least 1961 (7 pairs), reaching 22 pairs by 1984. The number of pairs attempting breeding has fluctuated since 1992 from four to 25 per year, with a mean of 17. Weather and the attentions of predators sometimes result in low breeding success.

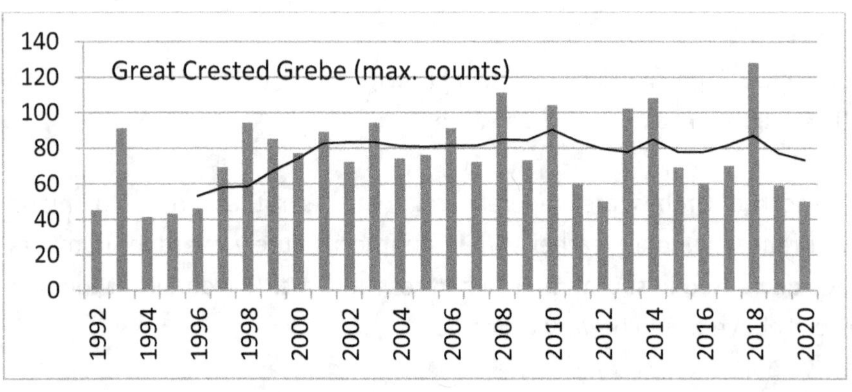

Slavonian Grebe   *Podiceps auritus*

A very rare winter visitor.

Seven firm records.

1976 Mockbeggar SE	Nov 7th
[2004 Ibsley Water	reported, Nov 20th]
2011 Ibsley Water	Feb 27th
2013 Rockford Lake	Jan 1st
2015 Ibsley Water	Oct 12th-13th; another, Dec 13th-Dec 31st (also on Rockford Lake)
2016 Ibsley Water	Jan 1st-Apr 12th (same)
2019 Ivy Lake	Nov 18th (photo)

This species is scarce but regular on the Hampshire coast, albeit in lower numbers in recent years, but is very rare inland in the county. 45 were recorded significantly far from the coast during 1951-92, but only five since, including the latter records above. There are no other records for the Avon Valley.

Black-necked Grebe   *Podiceps nigricollis*

Very scarce passage migrant, and occasional winter visitor. Formerly bred; may do so again.

About eight were recorded pre-1993.

1978 Mockbeggar Lake	Sep 3rd-6th; 2, Sep 27th
1983 Mockbeggar Lake	Aug 7th
1985 Mockbeggar Lake	2, Apr 23rd-26th (reported as pair)
1986 Spinnaker Lake	May 10th
1988 Mockbeggar Lake	Aug 21st-31st

Since then, the species has become more regular and frequent, has bred, and may now be expected annually.

1994 Ibsley Water	July 23rd-30th; Aug 26th-Sep 3rd (2 on Sep 1st)
1996 Ibsley Water	4 pairs plus one other bird May-July; 2 pairs hatched young, but only 2 fledged, from one of those broods; another pair built a nest
1996 Ibsley Water	present in the breeding season; also 3, Oct 26th
1999 Ibsley Water	present in the breeding season
2000 Ibsley Water	present in the breeding season
2001 Ibsley Water	present in the breeding season
2002 Ibsley Water	present in the breeding season
2003 Ibsley Water	present in the breeding season
2004 Ibsley Water	present in the breeding season

2004 North Somerley Lake	one pair bred; one young hatched but probably did not fledge
2005 Ibsley Water	Aug 25th (2 - one until 29th); Oct 22nd
2006 Ibsley Water	Apr 1st; Sep 13th; Dec 25th into 2007
2006 Ivy Lake	Nov 29th-Dec 17th (same as Ibsley Water above)
2007 Ibsley Water	From 2006 until Mar 6th; Oct 31st into 2008; Dec 12th into 2008
2007 Ibsley North	Mar 10th (same as first Ibsley Water above)
2007 Mockbeggar Lake	Dec 1st (same as third Ibsley Water bird above)
2008 Ibsley Water	From 2007 until Mar 18th (2); another, Feb 29th to Mar 21st; July 5th; 4, Aug 17th; Oct 7th; 2, Nov 8th into 2009; 2, Dec 14th (additional) until Apr 2009
2010 Ibsley Water	During Jan (2); 4, Mar 1st-26th (3 until Mar 30th); Sep 8th and 12th
2011 Ibsley Water	1-3 Jan until Mar 23rd; July 24th (and then regularly until the end of the year); another present Dec 18th
2012 Ibsley Water	1-4, Feb 21st-Mar 19th; 3, May 5th-6th; Aug 26th; Nov 17nd-Dec 24th (2, Nov 28th)
2013 Ibsley Water	Up to 6 at both ends of year
2014 Ibsley Water	7 early year; 3 late year
2015 Ibsley Water	4 early year – pre-breeding behaviour noted; 4 late year
2016 Ibsley Water	3 early year; 1 late year
2017 Ibsley Water	5 early year; Dec 18th-Mar 31st 2018
2018 Ibsley Water	Jan 1st-Feb 7th (in addition to bird above)

| 2019 Ibsley Water | 2, May 1st-2nd; Nov 25th-Mar 9th 2019 Nov 28th-Mar 31st; Dec 20th-Mar 31st; another, Dec 2nd |
| 2020 Ibsley Water | Jan 18th; 2, Mar 18th (additional birds to those from 2019 above); Dec 9th-31st |

Oystercatcher   *Haematopus ostralegus*

A scarce passage migrant, and has bred in recent years.

Following one on Feb 18th 1961, no more were recorded until 1985. Three were seen between then and 1988, and then there was another gap of eight years. Since then the species has been regular (not recorded in just two years). Five passage migrants during 1996-1999 were followed by a copulating pair on May 1st 2000, and a pair was present on at least one summer date the following year. After the last blank year on record (2002), single pairs were on territory during 2003-5, and in 2006 two pairs bred, but failed to fledge young. In 2008, successful breeding was finally proved, and two pairs fledged two young. Since then, breeding is generally attempted every year, with 2-3 pairs present. Productivity averages over 1 chick raised/pair, which is better than the Hampshire coastal average. Occasional passage and winter birds add to the occurrences.

Black-winged Stilt   *Himantopus himantopus*

A very rare visitor from southern Europe.

One confirmed record.

| 2008 Ibsley Water | May 10th |
| [2014 Ellingham Lake | Aug 2nd – rejected by BBRC] |

Inland records are very rare in Britain, and this is the only accepted inland Hampshire sighting out of a total of almost 30.

Avocet   *Recurvirostra avosetta*

A very rare visitor, increasing.

14 records, involving probably 20 birds.

1984 Mockbeggar Lake	Nov 17th
1995 Ibsley Water	June 20th
2007 Ibsley Water	Nov 17th
2010 Ibsley Water	Dec 4th
2011 Ibsley Water	Jan 8th-16th (presumed same as Dec 2010 bird); 4, Apr 20th
2013 Ibsley Water	Mar 23rd; Sep 18th; Oct 19th
2015 Ibsley Water	Mar 5th; May 2nd-3rd; Nov 24th
2016 Ibsley Water	2, May 11th
2017 Ibsley Water	Aug 28th; 3, Aug 31st (presumed different)

Inland records are not unheard of, and are plainly increasing in Hampshire, but are still rare.

Lapwing   *Vanellus vanellus*

A frequent winter visitor and migrant, and a scarce breeder.

Lapwings are frequently seen in flight at Ibsley Water, but grounded numbers are very variable, and the quality of the data is not good. Nonetheless, larger numbers once used the Lakes than is now usually the case. Flooding and freezing conditions in the Avon Valley still occasionally lead to large influxes. 1899 at Mockbeggar Lake on Jan 15th 1983 is the first four-figure record, and the all-time record is of 2000 on Feb 12th 1984. Five further 1000+ counts are noted between 1987 and 1995, but the highest counts since then (by some margin) have been 800 in Jan 2004, 1300 in Jan 2006, 805 in Sep 2006 and 749 in Feb 2011.

Breeding was first recorded in 2000 (five pairs), seven pairs raised two young in 2006, and by 2009 there were at least eleven territories in the area. However, breeding success is generally low, due to the attentions of Foxes and other predators.

Golden Plover   *Pluvialis apricaria*
Once a regular winter visitor, but now much rarer.

220 were seen flying north over Kingfisher Lake on Jan 2nd 1972, but there are no indisputable records of grounded birds until 1982. In 1984, 400+ were present on Dec 20th. Dated records then follow for five years from 1988-92, with large three-figure counts every year, and a maximum of 1250 on Dec 29th 1990. However, since that date there have been few records. There may be some missing data at play here, but they are undoubtedly a great deal scarcer than they once were. Indeed, the HOS database contains just 20 records of about 200 birds for 1993-2010, and from 2009 to late 2012, not a single record of the species was submitted to Going Birding. All records since 2013 are listed below.

2013 Ibsley Water   5, Jan 18th; 2 north, Mar 11th
2019 Ibsley Water   68 north, Feb 2nd; west, Oct 3rd

Grey Plover   *Pluvialis squatarola*
A very rare visitor.

Eight records of single birds.
1986 Mockbeggar Lake   June 15th
1996   Jan 1st; May 12th
2004   Nov 21st
2008   Apr 17th; May 14th
2010   one reportedly present at some stage!
2012 Ibsley Water   Feb 8th-10th

2014 Ibsley Water   Apr 22nd
2019 Ibsley Water   May 8th

Grey Plovers are rare inland, and are not recorded at such sites annually in Hampshire. The 2019 bird occurred on a red-letter wader day, with Turnstone, Knot and Bar-tailed Godwit all present – plus Black Tern, and Little and Bonaparte's Gulls!

Ringed Plover   *Charadrius hiaticula*
A scarce passage migrant and former breeder.

The first dated record is of two on July 26th/27th 1973. Two pairs bred at "Ellingham GPs" in 1975. Following autumn migrants in 1979 and 1983, and possible nesting in 1982, regular breeding was recorded from 1985. Possibly as many as five pairs nested. Certainly, that many did in 1987, with up to six in 1989, 1993 and 1994. In all, breeding was recorded in fifteen years between 1985 and 2007, and probably in 2009 as well. Other than breeding birds (and it is hard to disentangle the two classes of record), migrant Ringed Plovers are seen annually, mostly in Mar-May and Aug. The maximum count was of 22 on Mar 2nd 1991, and other day counts included 16 in May 1988 and 13 in Mar 1991, but singles and small parties up to three are commoner than larger groups by far: no count has exceeded six since 2010. High Arctic breeders (subspecies *tundrae*) probably comprise a significant proportion of the very late spring migrants, e.g. one on May 27th 2012, four on June 11th 2013.

Little Ringed Plover *Charadrius dubius*

A scarce passage migrant and regular breeder.

"LRPs" are among the very earliest of spring migrants to the Lakes. This has long been a classic site for the species as a breeder in the county. Under "natural" conditions, LRPs frequent sandy and gravelly bars and eyots on braided rivers, a habitat mimicked by (especially the earlier stages of) gravel extraction. Various lakes and other areas have seen breeding attempts over the years, but they are now regular only at Ibsley Water and a couple of other sites. The (remarkable) all-time maximum count is of 26 on July 23rd 2005.

As early as 1980, a remarkable 16 nests were found, built by 7-8 pairs. Four nests were successful, and eight young fledged. Breeding data between then and 2006 are fragmentary, but attempts were probably made every year. Success has been low, as a combined result of poor spring weather and the attention of Red Foxes. There are few safe breeding sites for LRPs (or other waders) on Ibsley Water, because of the lack of shingly islands.

2006 eight pairs bred; three pairs hatched young; three fledged
2007 eight pairs bred; four fledged
2008 eight pairs bred; two fledged
2009 five pairs bred; none known to have fledged

2010 six pairs bred; two fledged

2011 six pairs bred; one or two fledged

2012: up to seven birds present; breeding occurred

2013: no young fledged

2014: 2 pairs raised 4 yg

2015: 2 prs raised 5 yg

2016: 5 attempts, 2 prs raised 4 yg

2017: 5 attempts, 3 prs raised 5 yg

2018: 5 attempts, 2 prs raised (probably) 5 yg

2019: 5 attempts, no yg fledged

2020: 3 attempts, no yg recorded

Kentish Plover   *Charadrius alexandrinus*
A very rare visitor from southern Europe.

One record.
2003 Ibsley Water　　　　June 8th

This species is extraordinarily rare inland, and this is one of only two such records for Hampshire, out of an approximate post-1948 total of 60 birds. Kentish Plover is now a national rarity once more, and a repeat at Blashford seems most unlikely.

Whimbrel   *Numenius phaeopus*
A rare passage migrant, noted more often in recent years.

46 records of at least 130 birds. There have been four notable records of flocks of exactly ten birds, all since 2008. We still await a record of eleven or more!

1996	May 12th
1997	Apr 24th
1998	3, May 4th
2003	2, May 9th
2005	5, May 9th; 3, May 15th; July 22nd
2006	Apr 22nd; 2, May 1st
2007	May 1st; 6, May 7th; 6-8, May 17th; 4, July 20th
2008	10, plus 2 north, Apr 13th; 4, Apr 24th; May 9th
2009	Mar 30th; Apr 16th; 2, May 3rd; May 9th
2010	Apr 15th; Apr 24th; 10, Apr 25th; May 1st; July 25th; Aug 26th
2011	May 12th; May 15th; July 13th; 10, July 24th
2012	10, Apr 22nd; Apr 25th; 2, Apr 30th
2013	May 19th
2015 Ibsley Water	1-2 on five dates May 4th-14th; another, 23rd
2017 Ibsley Water	7, Apr 22nd; 3, May 17th
2018 Ibsley Water	Apr 24th
2019 Snails Lane	1 at night, Apr 2nd
2019 Ibsley Water	May 5th; 3, May 7th
2020 Snails Lane	4 at night, Apr 11th
2020 Ibsley Water	2, Apr 18th; 6, Apr 24th

Curlew   *Numenius arquata*

A rare passage migrant and winter visitor

34 records of 72 birds.

1993	Jan 4th
1994	9, left NE,
	May 8th
1995	July 31st; Dec 29th
1996	Jan 28th; 3, Aug 3rd
2005	3, June 6th
2006	Mar 8th
2007	July 11th
2008	flew north, Apr 13th
2009	Mar 1st; 2, May 15th
2010	Jan 17th; 3, Mar 14th; Mar 30th; May 1st; Aug 26th; Dec 23rd
2011	Apr 19th; Nov 10th and 14th (same)
2013 Ibsley Water	May 5th
2014 Ibsley Water	3, Apr 10th
2015 Ibsley Water	Mar 1st; Mar 30th; 4, June 3rd; June 16th; 1 south-west, Nov 24th
2016 Ibsley Water	7, Mar 3rd; Mar 5th; Nov 4th-6th; Nov 26th
2017 Ibsley Water	5+, Feb 26th (4 still present next day); 9, Mar 21st
2018 Ibsley Water	Mar 25th
2019 Ibsley Water	north after dusk, Feb 7th
2020 Ibsley Water	Apr 24th-25th

More were recorded during 2013-18 than in all previous years combined.

Bar-tailed Godwit   *Limosa lapponica*

A very rare passage migrant.

27 records of probably 47 birds.

1988	May 1st
1989	2, May 6th
1994	May 8th
1997	July 16th
2005	May 9th and 11th
2007	11, Apr 24th
2009	Apr 25th-29th
2010	May 4th and 8th
2011	Apr 29th, May 1st & 3rd
2012	10, Apr 30th; 3, May 1st
	(2 until 2nd)
2013 Ibsley Water	May 9th (2 next day)
2014 Ibsley Water	4, Apr 26th; Nov 21st
2015 Ibsley Water	May 1st-3rd; May 17th
2017 Ibsley Water	Apr 30th; May 5th
2019 Ibsley Water	May 1st; 2, May 8th
2020 Ibsley Water	Apr 6th
2020 Snails Lane	at night, Apr 13th; Apr 15th

All bar three of the records were of singletons, and all bar two were in spring. A strong concentration in the first half of May is notable.

Black-tailed Godwit   *Limosa limosa*

A scarce passage migrant and intermittently abundant winter visitor.

Prior to 2007, there were fourteen records of 38 individuals, with six records in spring, five in autumn and three in winter. A maximum of 18 was present on Mar 12th 1978, but records occurred in only eight years after that first record.

A dramatic turn of events in early 2007 saw a huge flock of 1200 arrive from the severely flooded Avon Valley, and roost on Ibsley Water (Feb 17th). The phenomenon was repeated on a smaller scale until Apr (207 roosted Apr 3rd), and then it seemed like business as usual had been restored, albeit with higher numbers and occasionally more substantial flocks. The rest of 2007 saw 3 records of 17 birds (2 spring, 15 autumn/early winter) from Oct-Dec, and 2008 saw 10 records of 85 birds (2 spring, 83 autumn), with flocks of 25 on Sep 9th and 40 during Sep 20th-30th.

But again, in early in 2009, the Avon flock found Ibsley Water to its liking, with a site record 1450 on Mar 6th, 1210 on 9th, declining to 500 on 13th and "just" 40 on 15th. A further eleven bird-days were recorded in autumn, but there may well have been some duplication, as most reports were of two birds.

2010 brought a smaller, but still historically impressive gathering of 400 in Jan, rising to 800 in Mar, but Apr brought just 14 bird-days. The Nov maximum was 106, and the peak was only 14 in Dec. 2011 was a year of relative calm once again, with 18 records of perhaps 100 birds, with a maximum of 61 on Feb 12th, but no gathering larger than seven in the latter half of the year. 700 circled, with 200 settling, on Dec 17th 2012. In 2013, a new record of 1500 was noted during Mar, and in 2015 a roost reached a maximum of 517 in Dec. After several years of sporadic presence, and none in 2020, a large flock built up at Ibsley Water in mid-Jan 2021, peaking at about 2000 on Jan 13th – a new record count.

It remains to be seen whether large flocks will again regularly return if Avon Valley conditions unsettle the Godwits there. But it seems unlikely that Black-tailed Godwits will be as rare as they once were at Blashford Lakes, at least for the foreseeable future. The birds are of the Icelandic breeding form, *islandica*.

Turnstone   *Arenaria interpres*
A rare passage migrant.

43 records of 77 birds.

Pre-1992	22 "Mockbeggar Lake" – not all accounted for
1980	3, May 7th; July 27th
1986	12, May 10th; May 18th
2003	2, July 27th
2005	3, July 28th; Aug 21st
2006	3, May 1st
2007	May 15th; June 3rd; July 24th
2008	Apr 26th; May 17th-18th; 2, Aug 2nd (one Aug 3rd)
2009	May 11th; May 19th

2010	June 1st; July 1st; July 22nd; 2 juvs, Aug 27th-30th
2011	May 22nd; 2, Aug 18th; 5, Aug 26th (two to 28th); 5, Sep 25th
2013 Ibsley Water	May 9th-11th (2 on final date)
2014 Ibsley Water	May 1st; July 27th; Aug 3rd
2015 Ibsley Water	June 1st-2nd; July 25th
2016 Ibsley Water	May 9th; May 21st
2017 Ibsley Water	Apr 30th; May 4th; May 15th-16th; May 20th; May 26th; July 30th-31st; Sep 2nd
2019 Ibsley Water	May 1st-2nd; 6, May 8th; May 20th; 2, Sep 26th
2021 Ibsley Water	July 30th

It is notable that ten of the records have involved more than one individual. Records are split almost exactly equally between spring and autumn.

Knot   *Calidris canutus*

A very rare passage migrant.

Ten records of 11 or 12 birds.

1991 Mockbeggar Lake	2, May 31st
1992 Mockbeggar Lake	May 24th
1994	Aug 23rd
2010	one reportedly present at some stage!
2011	Sep 4th-11th (2 on 6th-7th); Sep 19th-22nd
2013 Ibsley Water	Jan 24th-26th
2015 Ibsley Water	Apr 12th
2016 Ibsley Water	Sep 18th
2019 Ibsley Water	May 8th

Knot are rare inland anywhere, and the 2013 midwinter record is especially unusual.

Ruff   *Calidris pugnax*
A scarce passage migrant.

At least 54 records of at least 90 individuals. This species has become more regular in recent years. Of the dated birds, 36 were in spring, 38 were in autumn, and 11 were in winter.

1971	Feb 14th
1979	Jan 20th; 3, Dec 31st
1980	Aug 1st-7th
1981	2, Aug 17th-21st
1989	Jan 17th; Nov 25th
1990	recorded (no dates)
1993	♂, May 8th-9th and 22nd; 3, Sep 12th
1994	6, May 8th; May 14th-15th
1996	juv Sep 21st-22nd
1997	Mar 31st
1998	Mar 14th; 3, Mar 22nd; 2, May 4th; Sep 19th; Sep 27th
1999	4, Apr 19th; Sep 20th
2001	Apr 30th
2005	1-2 on six dates, Aug 28th-Sep 10th
2006	May 13th; ♂, Aug 30th; 3, Sep 27th-Oct 3rd
2007	Oct 2nd-6th
2008	June 7th; Sep 28th-Oct 11th
2009	May 15th; juv ♀ Oct 1st-7th
2010	juv ♀, Oct 14th

2011	Feb 12th; juv, Aug 26th-28th; juv, Sep 15th-26th
2012	1-4, Feb 25th-26th; Mar 2nd; Mar 31st; 1-3, Apr 2nd-5th; 2, Apr 8th-10th; Aug 20th-21st; Aug 26th
2013 Ibsley Water	2, May 12th; Aug 12th-15th; 1-3, Sep 11th-29th
2014 Ibsley Water	Mar 31st; Apr 4th; Apr 12th-15th; Aug 30th
2015 Ibsley Water	Jan 24th; May 4th; 7, Aug 30th; 1-2, Sep 7th-15th
2016 Ibsley Water	Oct 2nd; Nov 7th
2017 Ibsley Water	Apr 23rd-25th; Sep 5th-Oct 17th
2019 Ibsley Water	Apr 4th
2020 Ibsley Water	juv, Sep 22nd-25th

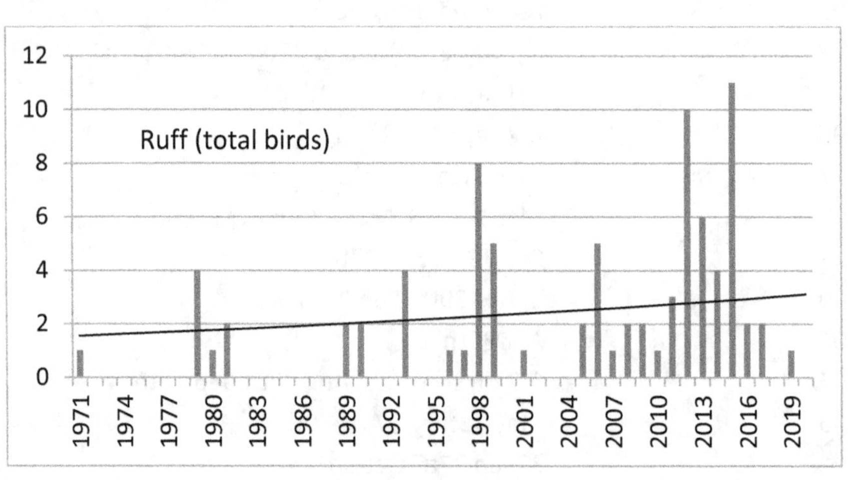

Curlew Sandpiper   *Calidris ferruginea*

A very rare passage migrant.

Seven records, all of single birds, and all but one in autumn.

1980 Mockbeggar Lake	July 29th
1993	May 13th
2005	Aug 26th; Sep 18th-25th
2010	Sep 8th; Oct 13th
2013 Ibsley Water	Sep 7th

Temminck's Stint   *Calidris temminckii*

A very rare spring (and autumn – once) migrant.

Eight records of seven or eight birds, all in May, bar one in July.

1980 Mockbeggar Lake	May 11th
1987 Mockbeggar Lake	2, May 16th-17th
1988 Mockbeggar Lake	May 14th
1994	May 14th
2005	May 28th
2007 Ibsley North Lake	July 24th
2009 Ibsley Water	May 6th and 13th (possibly same)

Sanderling   *Calidris alba*

A rare passage migrant, but near annual in recent years.

At least 25 records of at least 50 birds.

1983 Mockbeggar Lake	6, May 25th
1998	Apr 4th
2001	May 26th
2005	May 22nd
2006	May 21st

2008	two, May 25th-26th
2009	2, May 15th; 2, June 7th and 9th (one until 10th); July 18th
2010	5, June 1st
2011	May 7th, 15th and 30th – duplication possible; June 9th
2013 Spinnaker Lake	2, May 28th
2014 Ibsley Water	May 5th; May 11th
2015 Ibsley Water	Apr 28th; May 3rd; 18th; 31st
2016 Ibsley Water	7, May 21st
2017 Ibsley Water	May 14th; 17th
2021 Ibsley Water	3, May 16th

Six more were recorded pre-1992, but dates are not available.

Dunlin   *Calidris alpina*

A fairly frequent passage migrant and rare winter visitor.

Approximately 600 Dunlin have been recorded at Blashford Lakes, and this is undoubtedly the commonest of the passage wader species to occur at the site. Many of the more recent records, when the species has been recorded more frequently, are not precisely dated, or have been aggregated so their arrival date is not known. The first were 10 at Mockbeggar Lake on May 29th 1983, and this is a typical record: the species is distinctly more common in the spring than in the autumn. There are usually a few midsummer records, presumably of returning failed breeders. Winter records are quite rare, but far from unknown.

The dated records to 2012 (100+, of 280+ birds) are presented as an annualized graph below. The modal week, with 36 birds, runs from May 7th-13th. This week includes a flock of 22 on May 13th 1989, but the record flock was of 34 on the very unusual date of Feb 6th 1982, accounting for the unseasonal peak in the graph in week 6. A narrow 'second-best' flock of 33 occurred on a more expected date of May 8th 2021. Numbers have remained quite high in recent years (e.g. 42+ in 2013, 40+ in 2015).

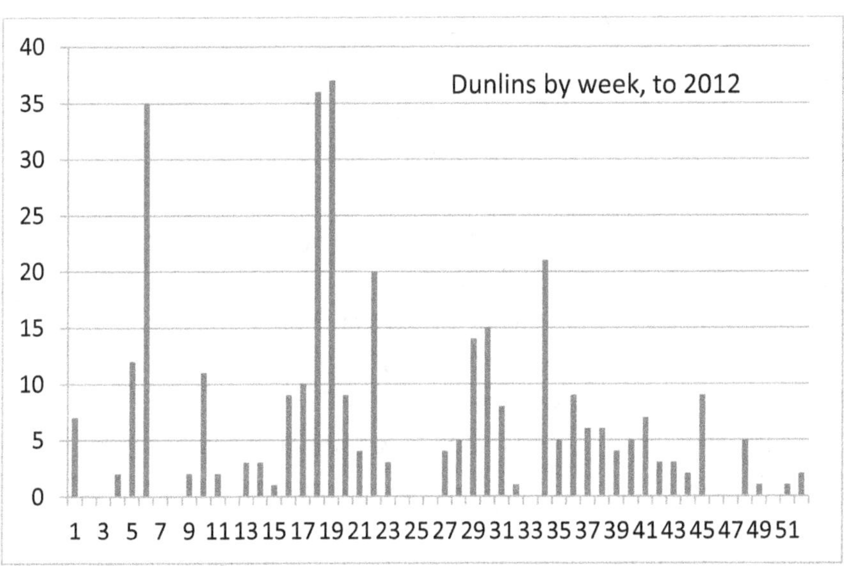

Little Stint   *Calidris minuta*

A rare passage migrant.

At least 27 records of at least 52 birds (possibly rather more). All but four records have been of autumn birds, the latter between Aug 10th and Oct 12th. The two June birds (in 1981) have not been classified as either spring or autumn birds, having occurred on midsummer's day!

1979	Sep 8th
1981	2, June 21st
1985	3, Sep 28th; Oct 2nd
1990	2, Sep 15th

1993	4, Sep 12th; 7, Sep 15th (presumed some same)
1994	May 22nd
1995	June 10th
1996	3, Sep 15th; 13-16, Sep 21st-25th (max Sep 22nd)
1998	3, Sep 12th; 2, Sep 19th
2000	juv, Sep 24th
2005	Aug 10th; up to 2, Sep 2rd-25th
2007	4, early Oct
2009	ad, Oct 11th
2010	Sep 29th-Oct 3rd
2011	Oct 7th and 12th (same)
2013 Ibsley Water	Sep 12th
2015 Ibsley Water	Apr 28th; Aug 13th; Aug 31st
2016 Ibsley Water	Oct 2nd-7th

Pectoral Sandpiper   *Calidris melanotos*

A very rare visitor from North America.

Two records of long-staying birds.

| 1981 Mockbeggar Lake | Aug 30th-Sep 20th |
| 2003 Mockbeggar Lake | Sep 14th-21st |

Of the 91 "Pec Sands" recorded in Hampshire, only about six have been inland, and a third of those, including the first, were at Blashford Lakes.

Long-billed Dowitcher *Limnodromus scolopaceus*

A very rare visitor from North America.

One record.
2009 Ibsley North Lake
juv, Oct 11th

This bird (see photo) was only the eighth Long-billed Dowitcher for the county, and the first for over twenty years. Sadly, it stayed for just one day.

Woodcock *Scolopax rusticola*

A rare but probably under-recorded winter visitor.

Dated records are as follows:

1996	Dec 27th
2002	Jan 4th
2006	Dec 27th
2007	Jan 17th; Dec 10th
2008	Nov 8th; Nov 24th; Dec 14th
2009	Dec 13th
2010	Jan 9th; 3, Jan 10th; 2, Jan 21st; 1+, Feb 6th; Dec 13th; Dec 22nd
2011	Jan 21st; Mar 4th; 2, Nov 20th
2012	Jan 9th; Jan 28th
2013 Snails Lane	One regularly at dusk during Feb/Mar
2014 Ibsley Water	Feb 11th

2016 Ibsley Water   Feb 22nd; Oct 21st; Dec 12th
2019 Ibsley Water   Feb 7th; Oct 6th

It is likely that Woodcocks are present regularly in winter, more visibly in hard weather.

Jack Snipe   *Lymnocryptes minimus*

A rare, but secretive and overlooked winter visitor.

10 dated records:

1995	Dec 9th
1996	Feb 23rd; Mar 30th
2002	Jan 3rd
2003	Jan 5th
2007	Nov 7th
2010	Jan 9th; Dec 5th; Dec 12th
2016 Ibsley Water	Dec 1st

There is not a great deal of accessible, suitable habitat for Jack Snipes at Blashford Lakes, and several of the very few records have related to birds flushed from exposed areas in cold weather. It is likely that the species occurs more regularly than is generally realised, but is nonetheless plainly very scarce at Blashford.

Snipe   *Gallinago gallinago*

A scarce winter visitor, but occasional large influxes.

The status of Snipe at Blashford Lakes is difficult to assess. There are remarkably few records, and those which exist generally refer to large counts. It is likely that these represent real influxes, which do occur in cold weather, and that the species actually occurs rather more frequently than the available records suggest. However, it is equally likely that many Snipe go unseen, given the large amount of difficult-to-view habitat. The all-time record count is of 105 on Dec 9th 1984, followed by 93 on Mar 22nd 1995. Only one other count has exceeded 50, and there have only been eleven double-figure counts since 2012.

Red-necked Phalarope   *Phalaropus lobatus*
A very rare passage migrant.

Two records.

2015 Ibsley Water	2♂♂, June 2nd
2021 Ibsley Water	June 28th

Another long-predicted species for the site finally fell to Bob Chapman, who 'only' had to wait another six years to find another!

Grey Phalarope   *Phalaropus fulicarius*
A very rare pelagic winter visitor.

Five certain records, with another reported.

2005 Ibsley Water	Jan 22nd
[2011 Ibsley Water	reported, Nov 16th]
2014 Ibsley Water	Nov 7th
2016 Ibsley Water	Sep 5th-7th
2017 Ibsley Water	juv, Sep 11th-14th
2018 Ibsley Water	juv, Sep 20th-30th
2021 Ibsley Water	juv/1w, Sep 27th-30th

Common Sandpiper   *Actitis hypoleucos*

**A fairly common passage migrant which has possibly oversummered,
and certainly overwintered.**

The data for this species are frustratingly sketchy, since it is scarce enough
to be recorded quite assiduously, but not for those data to be published in
disaggregated form! Nevertheless, it seems likely that there has been no
very substantive change in status over the years since the first published
record (15, Aug 29th 1977), with usually single-figure maxima in spring and
autumn (and presumably much turnover of birds on passage), and
occasional cases of overwintering (in about nine winters since 1983). One
possibly oversummered in 2008. The all-time record count is of 17 on Aug
17th 2003, but there were reportedly six double-figure counts before 1992,
and only one in the better-covered period since, so the species may be in
long-term decline at the site, as elsewhere.

Green Sandpiper   *Tringa ochropus*

A fairly common migrant and regular winter visitor.

This species has been annual since at least 1992, and probably longer, with
maxima ranging from 3-7 in spring and autumn alike, and occasional
midsummer records. It is commonly speculated that the very last
northbound Green Sandpipers probably "cross" with early (failed) breeders
heading south at sites such as Blashford Lakes! The largest passage count
on record is of 24 during Aug 2005. A few birds (generally 2-4, but 5 in late
Jan 2012) are usually present throughout the winter, except for very cold
spells, most often in recent years on Ivy and Rockford Lakes.

Redshank   *Tringa totanus*

A scarce passage migrant, winter visitor and intermittent breeder.

A record of 80 for an hour after dawn (which then left to the north) on Sep 21st 1980 is remarkable, and more than ever recorded at the site at one time since, by a factor of almost ten! The event coincided with a similar "grounding" of a migrant flock on the coast at Hurst on the same day. Other early dated records (1983-85) are of about 20 birds, all (oddly) in winter. The draining of Spinnaker Lake in 1987 saw a record 19-20 present during Mar/Apr, and there were further winter records in 1990-91, but evidence of passage as such was very sparse. Following eight on Apr 4th 1992, breeding was first recorded in 1994, when three pairs nested. Since then, as well as occasional (but surprisingly infrequent) passage birds (maximum 10, Mar 23rd 2005) and odd winter individuals, breeding has occurred in at least fourteen years (maximum 5 pairs in 1998), mostly around the shores of Ibsley Water. As with other waders, success is generally rather low.

Wood Sandpiper   *Tringa glareola*

A rare passage migrant.

32 records of 40 birds (15 in spring, 25 in autumn).

1988	Aug 13th
1989	2, May 28th
1990	May 5th; Aug 19th
1991	2, May 29th; Sep 14th

1992	3, May 23rd
2003	Aug 17th-18th; Aug 22nd
2005	May 28th; July 28th; 1-2, Aug 8th-10th; Sep 17th; Sep 25th
2006	Sep 2nd-3rd
2008	May 18th
2009	Aug 28th-31st; Sep 9th-10th
2011	Apr 28th; July 25th; July 28th-31st; 2, July 29th
2012	July 25th
2014 Ibsley Water	Aug 30th
2015 Ibsley Water	July 12th; July 25th
2017 Ibsley Water	May 20th
2018 Ibsley Water	Sep 15th; Sep 24th; Sep 29th-Oct 6th
2019 Ibsley Water	3, Apr 30th
2020 Ibsley Water	Apr 27th

It is notable that of the spring birds, no fewer than eight were during 1989-92. Spring passage is lighter than in autumn, and this pattern has been reinforced in recent years, although *very* recent records buck that trend.

Spotted Redshank   *Tringa erythropus*

A very rare passage migrant.

Seven records of single birds, all bar one on one date only.

1981	Aug 17th-21st
1988	June 25th
1990	Aug 19th; Sep 3rd
2003 Ibsley Water	juv, Aug 31st; juv, Sep 17th
2014 Ibsley Water	Aug 26th

Greenshank   *Tringa nebularia*

A scarce passage migrant and winter visitor (once).

Greenshanks have been recorded over 60 times at the Lakes, with one in winter (Jan 28th 1987), but the vast majority on spring (28%) and autumn (72%) passage. There are sufficient dated records to present a meaningful graph of annual occurrence. The record count appears to be of five on Aug 24th 2006.

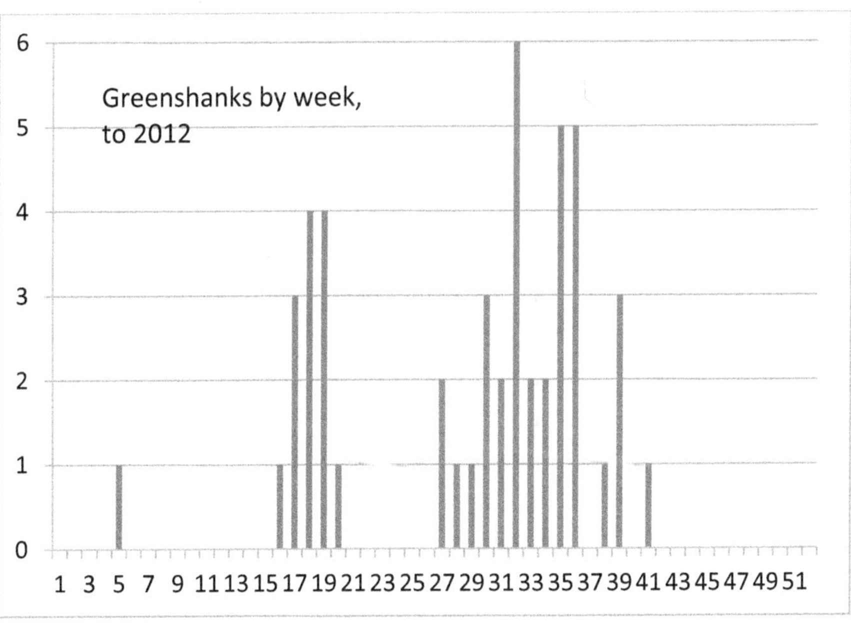

Collared Pratincole

A very rare visitor from southern Europe/the near East.

One record, only the second for Hampshire.
1987 Ibsley Water/   May 6th
     Mockbeggar Lake

A tremendous rarity in county terms, this was only the second of (so far) three Hampshire records. Another was reported on Jun 15th 2018 at Ibsley Water, but no details were ever submitted.

Kittiwake

A very rare pelagic visitor.

Ten records of eleven birds.

1981 Mockbeggar Lake	2, Apr 26th
2004 Ibsley Water	ad, Nov 18th
2006 Ibsley Water	ad, Apr 1st
2008 Ibsley Water	ad, May 16th
2009 Ibsley Water	ad, Jan 26th
2010 Ibsley Water	1cy, Nov 9th
2014 Ibsley Water	Feb 8th
2016 Ibsley Water	ad, Feb 8th
2019 Ibsley Water	ad, Mar 27th-29th; ad, Dec 13th

A rather peculiar spread of dates, and not all coming after especially stormy weather. It appears that a few Kittiwakes regularly cross land during passage periods.

Bonaparte's Gull   *Chroicocephalus philadelphia*

A very rare vagrant.

Three records, all within a very recent four-year period.
2017 Ibsley Water   2cy, Apr 17th- May 11th
2019 Ibsley Water   2cy, Apr 25th-May 12th
2020 Ibsley Water   2cy, Apr 20th-24th

This was the 15th gull species (plus four further subspecies) for Blashford, and leaves us awaiting a Laughing Gull to complete the "even vaguely probable" set! This astonishing sequence of 3 different first-summers in four springs is likely unequalled by any other site in Britain, and certainly by any inland site. The coincidence in dates is remarkable.

Black-headed Gull   *Chroicocephalus ridibundus*

A common visitor, sometimes in very large numbers in winter, and a recent breeding colonist.

Early records are very few. The first dated count is not until 1993, when a "small roost" developed on Ibsley Water (maximum 182, Dec 5th). It is perhaps safe to assume that this was a novelty for the site. Certainly, numbers have ballooned since then. In 1994, the roost peaked at 286, increasing to 680 the next year, both counts coming from Dec. In early 1996, 1520 were counted, rising spectacularly to 2400 by the end of the year. Numbers were somewhat lower in 1997 (although 4000 were counted flying over on Feb 9th, on a day when 1500 roosted), but spiked again the following Dec (1998) when 8000 roosted on the last day of the year.

This, along with an identical estimate on Feb 27th 1999, remains the record count. Despite numbers having stabilised at a much lower level, evening roosting by very large numbers of Black-headed Gulls has become a major feature of winter birding at Blashford in the last few years. Three to five thousand typically use the site, with peaks generally in Nov or Dec. 9000 were recorded roosting in early 2013, and a record 10,000 in Mar 2016.

In 2007, a colony was established at Ibsley Water, fledging 43 young. The next year, 60-80 pairs fledged 158 young, and numbers have grown every year since, reaching 254 pairs and 283 young by 2013. In 2016, a staggering 663 pairs nested. Predation and disturbance by foxes and Buzzards has caused a more recent decline.

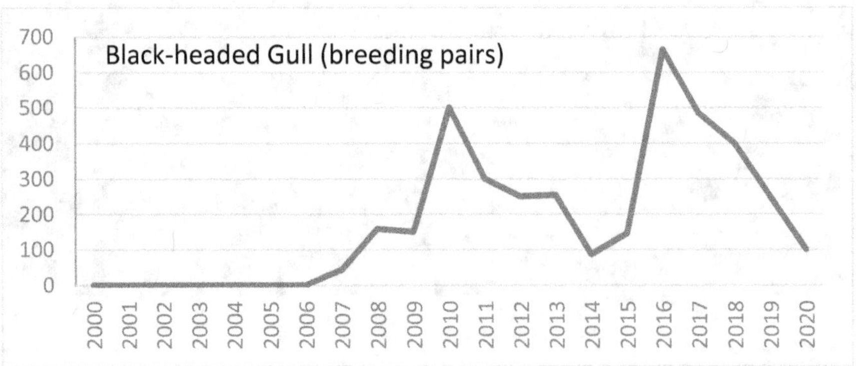

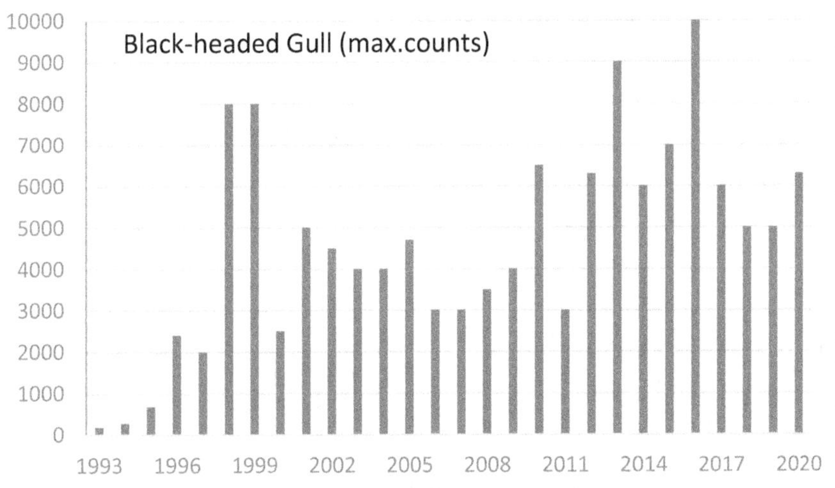

Little Gull   *Hydrocoloeus minutus*

A scarce passage migrant

Now an annual migrant. The first dated record is of one at Ivy Lake during
Sep 19th-25th 1983, but since then, spring birds have easily outnumbered
those in autumn, by 8:1. As elsewhere in southern England, there is a subtle
but distinct "double pulse" in spring, with peaks in late Mar and again in
mid-late Apr, with a few records as late as late May. The latest record Is of
two (an adult and a first-winter on Nov 24th 2002; they were first recorded
(assuming they were the same returning birds) on Oct 27th. The official
record count was of 10 on Apr 10th 2010 (all the tens) although an
unconfirmed report of 19 exists for Apr 3rd 2004 (two were present next
day). This last, very high count has not been included in the totals or graphs.
Winter adult birds were present on Dec 26th 1978 and at North Somerley
Lakes on Jan 5th 2003, the only records so far at that season.

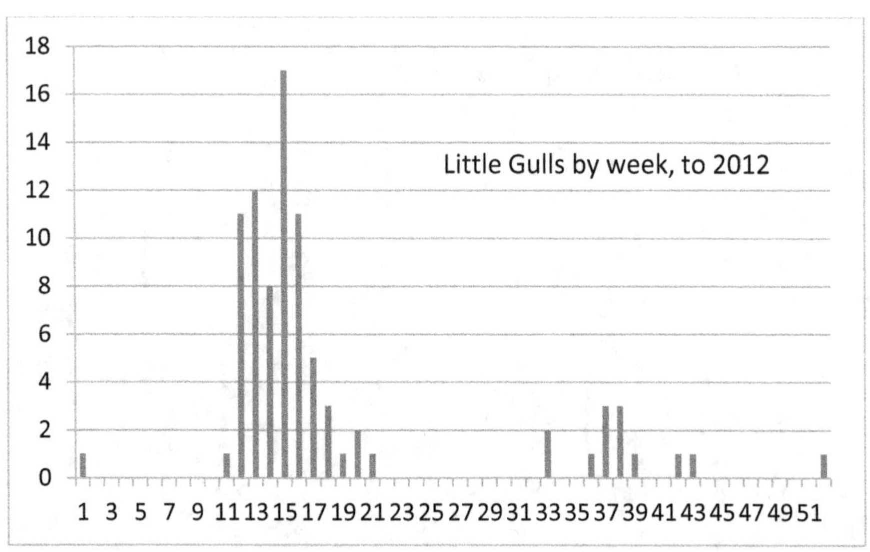

Franklin's Gull   *Leucophaeus pipixcan*

An extremely rare vagrant

One record.

2014 Ibsley Water   adult, Oct 19th; Oct 28th-Nov 24th

Located in flight (by veteran gull-god Rob Hume), this splendid second for Hampshire eventually pleased all comers in the nightly gull roost for over three weeks.

Mediterranean Gull   *Ichthyaetus melanocephalus*

Formerly a very rare visitor, now regular, and has bred.

The first for the Avon Valley was not until an adult was recorded at Blashford Lakes on Mar 11th 1990, and no more were seen until a juvenile on Aug 6th 2005. Two adults were noted in late 2006, and the species has been annual in increasing numbers since 2008. Typically, adults are located from time to time in winter gull roosts, and occasional late spring or early summer birds (perhaps failed coastal breeders?) show up, with occasional records of juveniles in summer. Ten were seen on Mar 12th 2010, and 30 on Mar 4th 2013.

Remarkably, two pairs established territories in the newly-established Black-headed Gull colony on Ibsley Water in 2011. One pair failed, but the other raised two young. This was the first inland breeding ever recorded in the county, and probably in the UK as a whole. Given that an absolute maximum of 88 bird-days had ever been recorded at Blashford Lakes prior to this, the record is little short of jaw-dropping. Coinciding with this auspicious event, a (then) record flock of 18 (12 of them adults) was present on Ibsley Water on July 10th 2011. 52 were present on Feb 29th 2016. This was further eclipsed by well over 100 present in early May 2017, at the same time as Bonaparte's and Little Gulls!

Further breeding attempts have occurred since, including on Spinnaker and Ivy Lakes. Totals have been:

2012	3 pairs present, no breeding evidence
2013	2 pairs present, no breeding evidence
2014	No evidence of breeding
2015	1 pair at Spinnaker Lake, raised 1 young
2016	3 pair at Spinnaker Lake, young raised
2017	3 pairs bred, raised at least 1 young
2018	2 pairs present, 1 successful
2019	1 pair bred at Ivy Lake, predated
2020	1 pair present, no evidence of breeding

Common Gull   *Larus canus*

A common (and sometimes abundant) winter visitor.

Records of Common Gulls at Blashford are easily the most unpredictable and variable of any of the commoner gull species. Birds may be distinctly rare for months at a time over some winters, only for large numbers to appear suddenly, and generally (but not always) when hard weather occurs. It is as yet unclear exactly where these birds come from, but presumably they are forced further south from their usual haunts and end up using Ibsley Water to bathe and roost.

The first dated record, of 200 on Dec 30th 1996 was regarded as very unusual, and indeed those kinds of numbers would still be notable, but hardly uncommon. 2000, however, brought an avalanche of Common Gulls. 960 were present on Aug 30th (an early autumn phenomenon not repeated since), and the site record count of 1825 soon followed on Oct 29th, with 960 still roosting on Nov 26th. 500 were counted on Dec 30th 2001, and 900 left the roost early on Jan 4th 2002. But numbers fell away rapidly in the next few years, with few large counts at all. The maximum for 2006 was only 18 birds, and in 2011 it was only 12!

However, cold weather influxes still occur, albeit on a smaller scale than in 2000-02. 200 were present in Feb 2009, 443 on Jan 14th 2010, 300 in Nov of the same year, and an impressive 743 on Feb 16th 2012. 1100 were present on Feb 7th 2015, and close 1000 on Jan 20th 2017.

Common Gulls are very rare outside the winter period. A first-summer on May 11th 2010 and one on June 25th 2020 were exceptional.

Ring-billed Gull   *Larus delawarensis*

A very rare visitor from North America.

Up to seven, all since
2009, one a regularly
returning bird 2014-19.

2009 Ibsley Water	2cy, Oct 11th; 1cy, Nov 6th (and prob. 15th)
2010 Ibsley Water	ad, Nov 7th
2011 Ibsley Water	2cy, Jan 22nd and 29th
2014 Ibsley Water	ad, Dec 23rd-Mar 7th 2015
2015 Ibsley Water	3cy, Jan 4th; returning ad, Nov 14th-Mar 25th 2016
2016 Ibsley Water	another ad, Mar 4th-12th; both returned during Nov/Dec, until mid-Feb 2017. [A third ad was strongly suspected in Mar.]
2017 Ibsley Water	returning ad, Dec 10th-Mar 31st 2018;
2018	returning ad, Nov 15th-Mar 27th 2019
[2021 Ibsley Water	Jan 4th-Mar 25th. Not yet assessed by HOSRP]

The first edition of this book stated "while the finder of Britain's first ever
Ring-billed Gull (in 1973) is now a 'regular' at Blashford Lakes, he has yet
to repeat the trick at this site, but few would bet against him!" He found
the 2014 bird, which returned every winter up to 2018/19.

Great Black-backed Gull   *Larus marinus*
An erratic visitor, usually in small numbers. Has bred.

For the most part, this species is a scarce visitor which occasionally joins winter gull roosts, and which puts in appearances at other times of the year on occasion. Generally, 1-3 birds are involved, but there are some remarkable older records of more. In 1995, an astonishing 125 were present on Dec 29th, having moved across from the then operational Somerley rubbish tip. This is far and away the largest count on record. Other "large counts" have included 12 on July 26th 1998, 51 on Dec 31st 1998, 13 on Dec 30th 2001, 10 on Jan 3rd 2002, 20 on Jan 11th 2004, 30 on Jan 7th 2006 and 20 on July 24th 2012.

In 2000, a pair established a territory on Ibsley Water and raised one chick. In 2001, they raised three young, but failed in 2002. In 2003, they hatched three young, but the nest was destroyed. No breeding behaviour has been observed since. This is a very rare and erratic breeder in Hampshire, and this remains the only instance of inland breeding in the county.

Glaucous Gull   *Larus hyperboreus*
A very rare winter visitor

One record.
2015 Ibsley Water   juv photographed, Jan 1st

This bird was present for a total of just ten minutes during two closely spaced visits at lunchtime, making it untwitchable. It became the 14th gull species to have been recorded at Blashford Lakes.

Iceland Gull   *Larus glaucoides*
A very rare winter visitor from the Arctic.

Eight accepted records, all since 2009.

2009 Ibsley Water	2cy, Jan 18th and Feb 26th
2010 Ibsley Water	2cy, Nov 21st
2011 Ibsley Water	2cy, Jan 1st and 2nd
2012 Ibsley Water	Jan 11th-12th; 2cy, Feb 17th-24th (presumed same)
2015 Ibsley Water	2cy, Jan 23rd
[2016 Ibsley Water	2cy, Feb 9th (not reported to HOSRP)]
2018 Ibsley Water	2cy *thayeri* Jan 28th-Mar 6th
2018 Ibsley Water	2cy, Jan 31st-Feb 9th; 2cy, Mar 26th and 31st (considered different)

Judging by the age classes, all the birds must all have been different individuals. Perhaps our "regularly returning" Caspian Gulls are not actually the same birds after all! Adult large "white-winged" gulls (i.e. Iceland or Glaucous) were reported on Oct 21st 2011 and Jan 16th 2012, but not specifically identified. A 2cy reported on Feb 19th 2014 and a 3cy reported on June 12th 2015 were found unacceptable by the HOS Records Panel, as was a juvenile bird reported as a "Kumlien's Gull" (*L. g. kumlienii*) by a highly experienced gull-watcher on Feb 2nd 2015. The juvenile "Thayer's Gull" of early 2018 was only the eighth for Britain, and was thus the rarest bird ever recorded at Blashford Lakes (unless you count White-throated Needletail, which you shouldn't).

Herring Gull   *Larus argentatus*
A common, mostly winter visitor.

Numbers of this species are generally much lower than those of its congener, the Lesser Black-backed Gull, but significant numbers still roost on Ibsley Water each winter, and loafing young birds are present year-round. 413 on Feb 23rd 1982 was a remarkable count, not matched until 1998, and generally the maximum was only 150-400 until then. 1500 on Sep 19th 1998 more than tripled the all-time record at the time, and a lean period followed. High numbers have again been recorded since 2009, when 1000 roosted on Dec 12th, a figure equalled on Oct 13th 2010. 345 (mostly first-summers) on Apr 26th 2010 was a notable record, as was 503 on Jan 22nd 2015. 500 were again counted that autumn, and in autumn 2016.

Birds of the form *L. a. argentatus*, which breed in northern Europe, probably occur from time to time, but the only dated records are of 2-3 on Nov 19th 2010,several on Dec 5th 2014, and "a few" in autumn 2015.

Caspian Gull   *Larus cachinnans*

A very rare but (recently) regular winter visitor.

Only quite recently split from the previous species, birders are now more aware of the identification criteria. Nonetheless, the species remains a very rare one in Hampshire, and Blashford's series of records is very noteworthy for an inland site. Precise dates are given below only for short stayers.

A minimum of 19 birds have been recorded, all since 2003

2003	ad, Dec 14th
2004	2 ads, Jan 2nd; one until 24th
2005	ad, Feb 17th
2007	Jan 21st; 1cy, Sep 2nd
2008/09	ad
2009/10	ad (same)
2010/11	ad (same); 2cy, Oct-Nov
2011/12	ad (same); possibly another Jan-Feb;
late 2012	ad (same), one date in Dec
2014	ad, Oct 27th
2015	3cy, Dec 6th
2016	2 2cys, Jan-Feb; 1cy, Dec-Feb 2017
2017	1cy, Nov-Mar 2018; possibly another, Jan
2018	ad, Jan-Feb, 4cy, Feb; 3cy, Feb; 1cy, Oct-Feb 2019
2019	another 2cy, Jan-Feb; 4cy, Feb; ad, Dec-Jan 1st 2020
2020	2cy, Feb

Caspian Gulls are thus now annual in very small numbers in winter. Most are 1cy or 2cy birds, but adults appear too and some birds may return in subsequent winters.

Yellow-legged Gull   *Larus michahellis*
A scarce but regular passage migrant and winter visitor.

The first were adults on July 28th and Nov 25th 1991, but no more were recorded until 1996, when eight occurred. 14 followed in 1997, 5 in 1998, 14 in 1999, 2 in 2000, and counts of 42 on two dates in 2001. In 2003, the species' status changed dramatically, with 65 on Nov 8th (and other high counts that autumn), and since then Yellow-legged Gulls have been a regular feature of winter roost gatherings. 2004 saw 207 bird-days, 72 of them in Oct, and although numbers have declined somewhat since about 2007, the record count of 72 was made in Oct 31st 2004. These days, typically, 10-15 birds join other large gulls in the roosting flocks. [On Jan 25th 2020, a 3cy "Azorean" type (*L. m. atlantis*) was claimed by a very experienced observer, but deemed "not proven" by BBRC.]

Lesser Black-backed Gull   *Larus fuscus*
A passage migrant and winter visitor, which roosts in large numbers.

Until the mid-1990s, Lesser Black-backed Gulls were irregular in occurrence. Their status has changed dramatically. Ibsley Water is now the biggest winter roost site in the county, by some margin. Apart from one or two in the winter months of 1967, a time when the species was generally scarce and very rare in winter, the first dated record is of 10 on July 1st 1989. 130 were recorded on Aug 30th in 1991. As late as 1995, a count of 25 on Dec 29th was considered interesting enough to be included in *HBR*. In 1996, the now familiar rapid autumn build-up began, with 55 on Oct 12th rising to 575 on 26th, and declining to just four by Dec 14th. Maximum counts grew, breaking 1000 (and 2000) in 1999, 5000 in 2002, 7000 in 2008, and peaking at an amazing 10000 in Sep and Oct 2009, a figure matched in Nov 2010 and 2013. Recent peak counts have been somewhat lower.

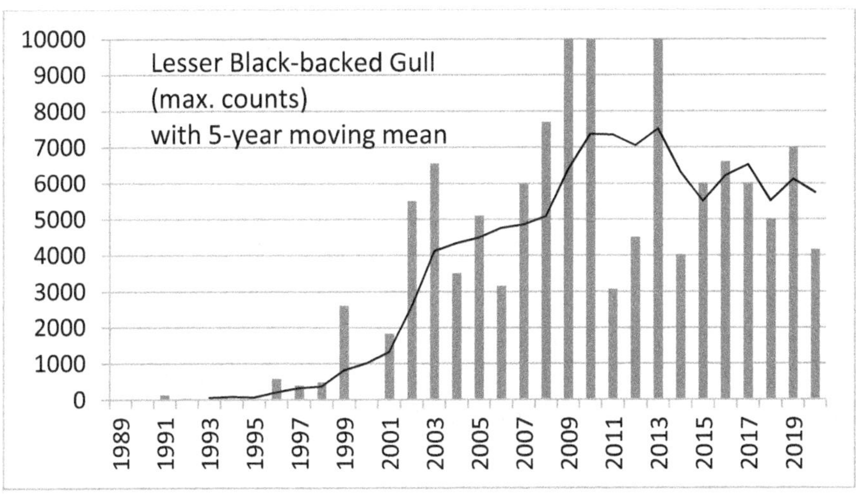

The large majority of birds are of the British-breeding form, *L. f. graellsi*, especially in mid-winter, but large numbers of European *L. f. intermedius* birds occur on passage. On more than one occasion, birds resembling the form *L. f. fuscus* have been observed, especially in Oct. This is a form not yet on the Hampshire list. On Jan 19th 2015, an exceedingly experienced larophile reported a bird strongly resembling *L. f. heuglini*, but the record could not be progressed.

A pair bred at North Somerley Lake in 2000, raising one chick. This was the first ever successful breeding for the county. Courtship behaviour has been noted on Ivy Lake tern rafts on May 3rd 2009, and a pair nested (unsuccessfully) on Ibsley Water in 2011.

Sandwich Tern *Thalasseus sandvicensis*
A rare spring visitor.

Eleven records of 26 birds.

1995	Apr 18th
2003 Ivy Lake	May 30th
2010 Ibsley Water	two, Apr 28th
2012 Ibsley Water	Apr 22nd
2014 Ibsley Water	Apr 7th; Apr 12th (possibly same)
2015 Ibsley Water	8, Sep 14th
2016 Ibsley Water	Mar 26th; 5, Apr 15th [another reported July 5th]
2017 Ibsley Water	Mar 30th
2018 Ibsley Water	4, Apr 4th

A very scarce bird inland in Britain.

Little Tern *Sternula albifrons*
A very rare passage migrant.

Eleven records of 17 birds.

1986	Apr 24th
2006 Rockford Lake	juv, Sep 24th
2011 Ibsley Water	May 1st-2nd (also reported a few days previously)
2012 Ibsley Water	Apr 23rd
2013 Ibsley Water	2, Apr 26th; 2, May 8th
2015 Ibsley Water	2, Apr 23rd; May 2nd; 2, July 12th
2017 Ibsley Water	2, May 4th
2019 Ibsley Water	2, June 2nd

Inland breeding is exceedingly rare in the UK, but is actually quite common in mainland Europe, and it is not impossible that the species might one day colonise, given appropriate habitat provision and protection. Certainly, the recent run of "pairs" in spring is encouraging!

Common Tern   *Sterna hirundo*
A fairly common passage migrant and regular breeder.

Common Terns appear regularly on passage at Blashford Lakes in both spring and autumn. 120 were recorded between 1971 and 1992, with a maximum of 39 on Aug 29th 1986. Other large passage counts include 30 on May 5th 2008. However, passage is often hard to detect, given the presence of significant numbers of breeding birds, notably on Ivy Lake (Spinnaker Lake used to hold breeding pairs, but the islands became too overgrown from 1993).

The first recorded nesting (and the first inland breeding record for the county) occurred in 1967, and pairs have nested regularly since then. 2-3 pairs were present during 1983-89, rising to five pairs in 1990, but as noted above, numbers then declined and breeding was not recorded in 1993-94. Provision of safe floating rafts on Ivy Lake has since produced an impressive recovery. Up to three pairs bred up to 2003, 8 in 2004, 8-10 in 2006, 15 in 2009 and a record 18 (raising a remarkable 42 young – 2.3 young per pair) in 2011. Productivity has generally been lower since, and predation and competition with Black-headed Gulls have been real problems.

2012	22 pairs	50 young	2.3/pair
2013	20 pairs	36 young	1.8/pair
2014	22 pairs	34 young	1.5/pair
2015	24 pairs	62 young	2.6/pair
2016	29 pairs	40 young	1.4/pair

2017	39 pairs	60 young	1.5/pair
2018	22 pairs	30 young	1.4/pair
2019	20 pairs	19 young	1.0/pair
2020	21-25 pairs	15 young	0.6-0.7/pair

A 2cy bird (the plumage formerly known as *'portlandica'*) was present in June and July 2015.

Arctic Tern   *Sterna paradisaea*
A very rare passage migrant.

36 records of at least 121 individuals.

1977	Ivy Lake	"autumn"
1983	Ivy Lake	Sep 19th-25th
1985		May 8th
2004		Aug 29th
2005		July 23rd; Aug 25th
2006		2+, May 1st
2008		3, Apr 30th; May 1st; May 3rd; Aug 19th
2010		Apr 13th; Apr 30th-May 1st
2011		juv, Sep 6th; 5 ads, Sep 9th; juv, Sep 12th-14th
2013	Ibsley Water	1-3, Apr 22nd-26th; 1-2, May 9th-11th (one 2cy)
2014	Ibsley Water	45, Apr 23rd; Apr 27th; Apr 29th; May 13th
2015	Ibsley Water	Apr 29th; May 5th; 2, May 18th; 3, Aug 7th; Aug 31st
2016	Ibsley Water	May 14th; Aug 6th
2017	Ibsley Water	May 14th; 2 juvs, Sep 10th
2018	Ibsley Water	25, Apr 15th

2019 Ibsley Water   2, Apr 27th; May 10th
2020 Ibsley Water   2, Apr 21st; 2 juvs, Aug 25th

It is entirely likely that Arctic Terns have been substantially overlooked at Blashford Lakes until recently, but they are, nonetheless, scarce and notable inland. The flock of 45 in 2014 was remarkable.

Whiskered Tern   *Chlidonias hybridus*
A very rare visitor from southern Europe.

One record.
1988 Mockbeggar Lake   2 adults, May 14th

The first of only two "non-singleton" county records. Perhaps overdue for a reappearance. There were high hopes when one spent a protracted period at nearby Longham Lakes in spring 2021!

White-winged Black Tern   *Chlidonias leucopterus*
A very rare passage migrant from eastern Europe.

One confirmed record and an earlier report.
[1980 Mockbeggar Lake   2 flying south, May 3rd; never submitted to
                             or accepted by the BBRC]
1991 Spinnaker Lake   juv, Sep 22nd-25th

This is a very likely candidate for another occurrence, especially now that Black Tern, the classic carrier species, is commoner at the Lakes than it once was.

Black Tern   *Chlidonias niger*

A scarce passage migrant, mostly in autumn. Significant interannual variations, and very occasional large flocks.

There have been over 100 records of this species, many of them of small parties or larger flocks, totalling approximately 320 individuals. The first dated record was on Sep 12th 1981, but there were as many as 22 on Sep 15th 1982. This flock was only just eclipsed by 23 on Aug 31st 1986, a record which stood for 25 years, until an amazing 49 appeared at Ibsley Water on Sep 24th 2011.

A Peregrine appeared during the latter's visit, and all the Terns flew up into a tight defensive ball and flew south, bar one which spent ten minutes fleeing the predator's spectacular attentions. It did escape in the end! It is worth noting that this spectacular flock did not all appear at once, but built up quite slowly over the day, indicating that Black Tern passage can and does occur throughout the day. This further suggests that some are missed, or assumed to represent the same bird, when in fact more are involved.

Double figure counts have been made on just two other occasions (16, Aug 28th 1986; 13, Aug 31st 2008). Black Terns were seen at Blashford in 21 years during 1982-2011, missing just three years between 1991 and 2011, and have been annual since 2003 (except 2014), showing a strong increase in numbers since about 2006.

Up to 2012, 26 dated records (42%) of 76 birds (27%) were noted in spring, compared with 36 records (58%) of 201 birds (73%) in autumn, confirming the greater likelihood of larger groups appearing at the latter season. The graphs below shown (i) the seasonal distribution of records (note the interesting late summer peak, relating to failed breeding adults, ahead of the main autumn passage of adults and juveniles migrating together) and

(ii) the number of birds recorded in each year. While occasional large counts do influence the latter considerably, there does seem to have been a sustained and genuine increase in recent years, unlike at many coastal sites in the county. 2020 was a blank year, however.

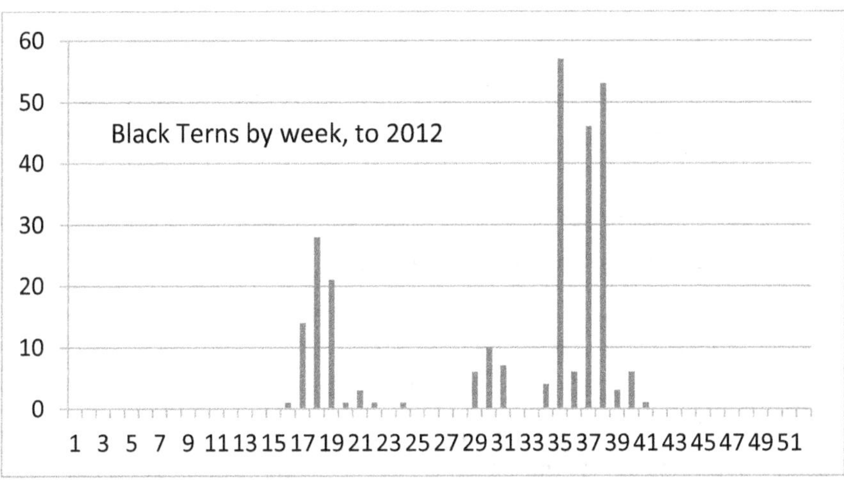

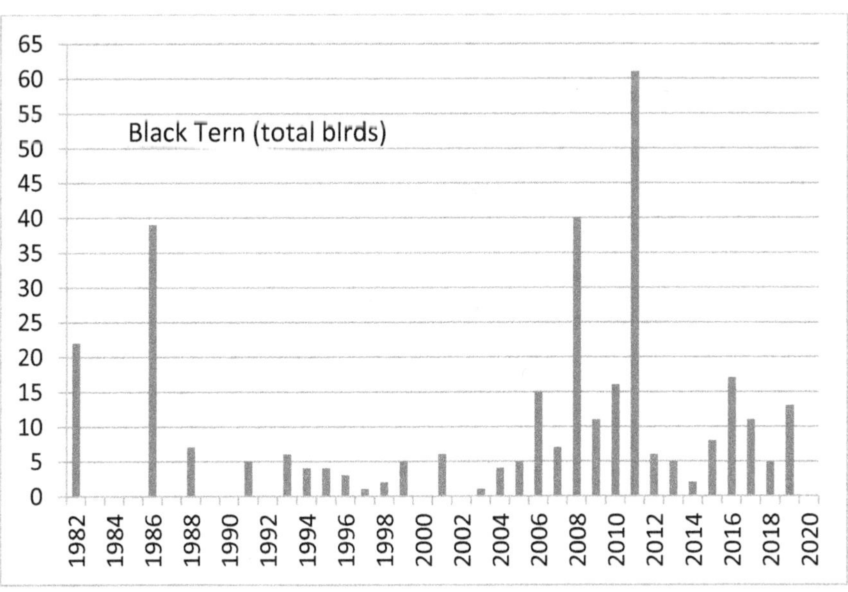

Arctic Skua   *Stercorarius parasiticus*

A very rare pelagic visitor.

One record.
2007 Ibsley Water   Nov 6th

Long-tailed Skua   *Stercorarius longicaudus*

A very rare pelagic visitor.

One record, among the most extraordinary of them all for the site.
2010 Ibsley Water   3 juvs flew south, Sep 23rd

Only the third inland record for Hampshire (the previous being from Crawley in 1891 (!) and Fleet Pond in 1991), and the first county record of more than two birds in a day. A superb reward for the hours of observation by Bob Chapman, the Warden of the Reserve at the time.

Little Auk   *Alle alle*

A very rare pelagic visitor.

One record.
2016 Ibsley Water   Nov 3rd

A long overdue addition to the Blashford list.

Red-throated Diver · Gavia stellata

A very rare winter visitor.

Four records.

1993 Ibsley Water	Jan 4th (oiled)
1993 Spinnaker Lake	Dec 23rd
1996 Ibsley Water	Feb 23rd
2003 Somerley Lakes	Feb 27th-Mar 2nd

Red-throated Diver is, nationally and proportional to its absolute abundance, the least likely of the three divers to be found inland. It is comfortably the commonest of the three regular species in British (and indeed Hampshire) coastal waters.

Black-throated Diver · Gavia arctica

A very rare winter visitor.

Three records.

1978 Spinnaker Lake	Feb 26th
1984 Hucklesbrook N. Lake	Dec 9th, shot
2016 North Poulner Lake	Nov 29th-Dec 14th when moribund

Despite the comments under Red-throated Diver above, this is the rarest of the family at Blashford Lakes, and it was a long wait of over 30 years for the most recent.

Great Northern Diver *Gavia immer*

A very rare winter visitor.

Ten records.

1954 Site unknown	Jan 3rd (found dead)
1995 Ivy Lake	2cy, Jan 14th-18th
1995 Spinnaker Lake	Dec 16th-Jan 14th 1996
2007 Rockford Lake	Nov 30th
2008 Ibsley Water	Nov 9th
2010 Ibsley Water	Nov 11th-12th
2012 Ibsley Water	Nov 13th
2014 Ibsley Water	Jan 26th; Nov 3rd
2020 Ibsley Water	Dec 5th

The greater frequency of records in recent years is notable, and in line with an increase in the numbers of Great Northern Divers recorded along Hampshire's coast in winter. Late autumn has clearly emerged as the best time to find a Great Northern at Blashford! Of the three "common" diver species, this is generally the one most prone to straying inland. The first record is the very first firmly dated record of *any* species for the area treated here.

Leach's Petrel *Hydrobates leucorhoa*

A very rare pelagic visitor.

One record.
2009 Ivy Lake/Ibsley Water   Nov 29th

This bird occurred the same day as a major coastal wreck of this species, when about 89 occurred in Hampshire, which is the all-time day record for the county.

Fulmar   *Fulmarus glacialis*

A very rare pelagic visitor.

One record.
1989 Mockbeggar Lake   Sep 13th

A very remarkable record, but Fulmars are known to wander inland from time to time. Bizarrely, the peak time nationally for such occurrences seems to be in late spring and early summer.

White Stork   *Ciconia ciconia*

A very rare visitor from southern Europe; feral population now established in southern England.

One record.
2008 Ibsley Water   flew south, May 30th
[2020 from Ibsley Water   well out of area to north, Apr 6th]
[2020 Snails Lane   July 10th]

This remains a very rare bird in Hampshire, with just 48 records. Proof of a future bird being wild will be near impossible given the establishment of a released population at Knepp in Sussex. One was at nearby Ellingham in the Avon Valley during Sep 21st-22nd 2010.

Gannet   *Morus bassanus*

A very rare pelagic visitor.

One record.
2010 Ibsley Water   sub-adult south, Aug 26th

The observer is unknown, and the record survives only by dint of someone writing it in the hide log. They wrote "juv" and then crossed it out and wrote "sub-ad", suggesting a degree of birding aptitude, and the record was deemed acceptable by HOS. Further credibility is perhaps added by one seen over Farnborough on Aug 23rd 2020!

Cormorant   *Phalacrocorax carbo*

A common visitor, especially numerous in winter.

Cormorants are virtually ever-present in small numbers at Blashford Lakes, but at times their numbers grow spectacularly, and hundreds may be present loafing and occasionally feeding, especially on Ibsley Water's islands. The first dated record is of just 10 on Kingfisher Lake in late Jan 1970, and the maximum recorded in 1984 was still only 18. But numbers using the Avon Valley for feeding have increased hugely since, in line with other inland sites. It is likely that many, if not most of these birds are of the so-called "continental" form, *P. c. sinensis*. Certainly, close scrutiny of Cormorants at Blashford indicates that this form is, at least sometimes, in the majority. Absolute proof finally came of the occurrence of *sinensis* with a colour-ringed bird in July 2012. It had been ringed at Lac de Grand-Lieu (France), the very same spot where "the" Great White Egret was colour-marked! Conversely, a Cormorant ringed on the Isle of Man (of the form *carbo*) was sighted at Blashford during Sep-Oct 2011. It had been ringed as a chick on June 9th of the same year, and is the bird in the photo above. Other field records of ringed Cormorants have proved arrivals from the Bristol Channel area.

79 were present at once in 1986, and 138 in Feb 1989. This record was not broken until Dec 2003 (157), but an even higher count (272) was made on Dec 21st 2010, and 269 were present on Mar 6th 2011. The all-time record is now 331 (Sep 28th 2016).

A pair (of unknown form) bred on an island in Ibsley Water in 2010, and there is a strong possibility that full-scale colonisation by tree-nesting *sinensis* Cormorants will occur at some stage in the future.

Glossy Ibis   *Plegadis falcinellus*

A very rare visitor from southern Europe.

Two records.

2010 Ibsley Water	Sep 18th
2013	flew north, Jan 27th
2021 North Poulner	9 south, Oct 22nd

These are excellent records for any inland site, but this species has seen a dramatic increase in Britain in recent years. The October 2021 flock (subject to ratification by HOS) constituted the largest group yet seen in the county.

Spoonbill   *Platalea leucorodia*

A very rare visitor.

Three (or perhaps four) records.
2007 Ibsley Water   east, Dec 30th or 31st
[2014 Ibsley Water   in flight, June 14th - unsubmitted]
2016 Ibsley Water   Aug 17th
2017 Ibsley Water   Oct 15th-16th

As with other southern herons and their allies, there has been a distinct increase in recent years, and there have been semi-regular records of late from elsewhere in the Avon Valley. More can be expected.

Bittern   *Botaurus stellaris*

A rare, but regular winter visitor. Less frequent than a decade ago.

The first record was on Snails Lake as recently as Jan 6th 2002. Probably the same bird was seen at Ivy Lake on Jan 20th of the same year. Bitterns are known to be highly site faithful in successive winters, so it is a matter of conjecture how many have ever occurred, but they have been missed in only three winters since that date, and numbers have increased. Two were suspected to be present in early 2003 and late 2007, and certainly there was more than one in early 2008. Three were confirmed for the first time during Feb 2009, and four were counted on Jan 26th 2011. Up to three were present in winter 2011/12, until Mar 17th, and up to two in late 2012, from the early date of Oct 25th. While still regular in winter since, only one has been present at a time, except on a couple of dates.

Almost all recent sightings have been made from Ivy North Hide, where the birds frequent the dense reed and *Glyceria* beds. They are best observed shortly before dusk, when they frequently call and sometimes climb the reeds prior to going to roost. In hard weather, they may be forced out of their preferred habitat. A very early bird was on Ivy Silt Pond on Sep 19th 2021. At least one has been seen wandering disconsolately around the frozen, flooded woodland along the Dockens Water.

Cattle Egret   *Bubulcus ibis*
A very rare visitor from southern Europe.

Seven records of 10 birds.

1994 Snails Lake	roosted, July 14th & 15th
2015 near Snails Lake	flew south, Sep 2nd
2018 Ibsley Water	2, Aug 30th; 3, Sep 13th; 1 of same 15th, 19th; Nov 13th
2019 Ibsley Water	2, Sep 23rd

This species has become much commoner in England and Hants since 1994, and now breeds in the county. It is now not infrequently found in the Avon Valley.

Grey Heron   *Ardea cinerea*
A common visitor, occasionally in large numbers.

Grey Herons have used Blashford Lakes for as long as anyone can remember, but numbers grew significantly in the late 1980s. 25 were noted on Oct 2nd 1988, but even this good count was totally eclipsed by 137 in Sep 1989, on a semi-drained and very low Mockbeggar Lake. Annual maxima failed to reach even half that figure until 2005, when 79 were present on Aug 21st. The all-time record was approached on Sep 26th 2010, when a staggering 120 were present, mostly on Somerley Lakes. 125 were present on Sep 27th 2015.

A breeding colony is recorded as having existed "at Blashford" from at least 1984-1990, but it is not clear whether it was located within the area treated here, and it certainly no longer exists.

Purple Heron   *Ardea purpurea*
A very rare visitor

One record. Perhaps this species should have been predicted more widely, but the date is relatively unusual.

2014 Ivy Lake   photographed, July 4th

Great White Egret   *Ardea alba*
A rare but regular visitor – at least since 2003.

There have been numerous records since 2003, and one has been resident from late summer until early in the new year since 2005. The first record was of one at Mockbeggar Lake on Aug 21st 2003; it reappeared on Oct 31st and was seen until Jan 25th 2004. A new colour-ringed bird (which was ringed as a nestling at Lac de Grand-Lieu, Vendée, France, on May 3rd 2003 – a site 422 km almost exactly due south from Blashford) then took up its mantle, appearing at the Lakes from Nov 5th until Jan 23rd 2005. It returned for a second "winter" on July 17th, and was joined by a third bird for the site on Oct 11th. On July 3rd 2006, the regular bird returned, this time with an unringed bird (possibly the 2005 bird?) in tow, but the latter departed on July 16th, leaving "Walter White" (photo above) in place until Jan 20th 2007. The now familiar pattern of early year disappearance and high summer reappearance has been repeated by this bird every year since. It has been remarkably predictable in its departure date, which is almost always at the very end of January.

Another bird was present in late 2016, it or another during Jan/Feb 2017, with a third on Feb 9th, and finally another on Sep 25th. Since 2017, up to three have been seen at various times, generally around Ibsley Water and/or Mockbeggar Lake. A record five were seen in Nov-Dec 2020.

Like a ghost, Walter disappeared into memory sometime during the early months of 2020. He had reached the venerable age of almost 17, which easily exceeds the longest-lived Great White Egret recorded by EURING, the European bird-ringing and -marking database (at 13 years 9 months).

Little Egret   *Egretta garzetta*

A frequent but rather erratic visitor.

The first record was of one at Mockbeggar Lake on Aug 17th 1993, and multiple records became annual from 1995 onwards, coinciding with the colonisation of Britain by Little Egrets as breeders. By 1997, records in the Avon Valley were too numerous to be recorded individually, and birds could be seen very regularly at Blashford Lakes. By 2007, 50 bird-days were recorded in Nov alone. Despite the record count being of 50+ on Nov 17th 2011, there is a strong suspicion that the species has become significantly less common and regular in very recent years, possibly as a result of a succession of very cold winters. A roost count of 34 at Linbrook West on Dec 18th 2017 was notably high.

Osprey   *Pandion haliaetus*

A scarce passage migrant. Much increased, but oddly scarce in very recent years.

The first record which can be located is of one on Oct 31st 1976, at Kingfisher Lake, but no more were recorded (officially at least) until 1996, since when Ospreys have been noted in all but two years, and annually since 2005. 1996 saw eight "in the area" (which may include birds outside the area treated by this report), and there were five the following year. Up to five (or perhaps more) have been recorded in most recent years, with two on two occasions.

Recent bird-days per year are tabulated below:

2014	2015	2016	2017	2018	2019	2020
11	31	14	11	6	4	14

The apparent 'decline' since 2015 is very odd, given the Poole Harbour reintroduction project and continued growth of the British population. Perhaps Fishlake Meadows in the Test Valley is attracting 'our' Ospreys these days? Observer complacency and failure to report is another possibility.

The earliest date was Mar 26th 2008, and the latest was that of the 1976 bird (Oct 31st). Perhaps one day Ospreys might even breed at Blashford? A nesting platform was erected on the east side of Ibsley Water in early 2013, so we can dream… For now, it seems likely that most of our migrants are Scottish breeders, as confirmed by a colour-ringed adult on Apr 6th 2012, which had been ringed as a nestling in July 1997 in the Rothiemurcus Forest, Speyside, making it over 14 years old.

Honey-buzzard   *Pernis apivorus*

A rare summer visitor and passage migrant.

15 records.

1998 Ibsley Water	June 6th
2004	2 flew west, Aug 20th
2006	Sep 26th
2007	July 22nd
2008	flew south, June 29th; July 12th and 20th; Aug 16th – duplication possibly occurred
2009	May 13th
2011	Aug 9th
2013 Ibsley Water	May 30th
2014 Ibsley Water	Aug 12th
2017 Ibsley Water	Aug 1st
2018 Ibsley Water	Oct 8th

Better observer coverage probably accounts for most of the apparent increase since the first in 1998, since "HBs" breed no more than a few kilometres away in the New Forest.

Sparrowhawk   *Accipiter nisus*

A regular visitor.

There are no meaningful data in existence for this species, but Sparrowhawks are frequent visitors, often causing havoc among smaller birds, especially around the various feeding stations in the area.

Goshawk   *Accipiter gentilis*
A rare but probably overlooked visitor. Increasing.

About thirteen individuals have been recorded.

2000 Somerley Lakes	Mar 3rd
2010 Ibsley Water	Dec 18th and 22nd
2011 Ibsley Water	juv ♀, Aug 17th; juv ♂, Sep 8th
2013 Ibsley Water	Sep 2nd
2017 Ibsley Water	Mar 2nd; Mar 24th
2017 Hucklesbrook Lake	Aug 20th
2018 Ibsley Water	Apr 22nd & 23rd
2019 Ibsley Water	Jan 30th; Mar 29th; [probable, Sep 3rd]
2020 Ibsley Water	displaying pair, Mar 1st
2021 Ibsley Water	juv, Aug 5th

With a now well-established breeding population in the New Forest, it seems surprising that just nine firm records exist for Blashford Lakes. It is probable that some are being overlooked.

Marsh Harrier   *Circus aeruginosus*
Formerly a very rare passage migrant, now a regular visitor.

About 20 records to c.2017, then a rapid change in status.

2009	♀, May 12th; Sep 2nd and 13th, Oct 2nd (probably all same); Oct 13th
2010	♀/immature, Mar 26th; immature, Sep 2nd
2012	flew high east, May 6th
2013 Ibsley Water	♂, flew west, Mar 24th; flew south, Sep 30th
2014 Ibsley Water	Jan 6th; ♀ flew south Mar 31st
2015 Ibsley Water	May 7th; Aug 27th-28th

2016 Ibsley Water	May 8th; intermittently Nov 4th-17th (2 on 14th)
2017 Ibsley Water	Feb 11th; July 25th; Aug 20th
2018	Fifteen records, all autumn/winter
2019	20+ records, two in summer
2020	11 bird-months, Jan-Aug

Clearly a species undergoing a status change. Breeding now occurs in the Avon Valley and yet more Marsh Harriers are to be expected at Blashford.

Hen Harrier   *Circus cyaneus*
A very rare winter visitor.

About 22 records, probably relating to some 17 individuals.

1989	Dec 3rd, 8th, 10th and 16th (same)
1993	♂, Nov 21st
1997	Jan 30th; Dec 7th
2003	Mar 9th
2006	flew east, Dec 9th
2007 Ibsley Water	Jan 25th; Dec 28th-29th
2009 Ibsley Water	Jan 2nd and 24th; Feb 8th; Oct 8th
2010	ad ♂, Jan 15th and 31st; Feb 13th (presumed same); Mar 26th; Apr 4th; Nov 18th
2013 Ibsley Water	ad ♂, Mar 16th (possibly outside boundary); ringtail, Sep 15th
[2014 Ibsley Water	2, May 17th – a very late date. Was Montagu's fully ruled out? Never published by HOS]

This species is in serious decline in southern England, and the lack of records since 2014 at least is not really a surprise.

Red Kite   *Milvus milvus*

Formerly a rare visitor, now frequently seen. First recorded 2004.

Twenty-three records, relating to about 26 birds, up to the end of 2014. A substantial and sustained increase since. With the firm establishment and continued growth of southern English populations, the curve surely points only upwards for the future.

2004	Sep 19th
2007	May 22nd
2008	Apr 6th and 10th; 5, in groups of 3 and 2, May 4th; June 6th
2009	Feb 22nd; Apr 11th and 25th; May 2nd
2010	Apr 4th; Apr 10th; Apr 17th; May 27th-28th and 30th
2011	May 14th-15th
2012	Feb 18th; May 5th; May 14th; June 17th; Nov 5th
2013	Apr 27th, May 17th (2)
2014	June 13th
2015	15 records, Jan-Jun – doubtless some duplication
2016	Over 40 sightings, throughout the year, including up to 7 on two dates
2017 onwards	Now regular – max. 5 west May 10th 2020 during a major movement in the south of England

Black Kite   *Milvus migrans*

A very rare visitor from southern Europe.

Two records.

[2009 Somerley Estate   May 31st – seen *from* Ibsley Water!]
2011 Ibsley North Lake   Apr 25th
2016 Ibsley Water   Apr 30th, photographed

The 2009 near-miss is included here [in square brackets] for completeness!

White-tailed Eagle   *Haliaeetus albicilla*

An extremely rare vagrant, but now reintroduced locally.

Two records of wild birds. Post-2018 records will be regarded as
reintroduced birds, unless proven otherwise.

2018 Ibsley Water   juv, Dec 18th and 21st
2020 Ibsley Water   [probable, Feb 26th]; Mar 1st
[2021 Ibsley Water   Apr 10th]

These were the last demonstrably "wild" White-tailed Eagles to occur in
Hampshire: a reintroduction project began on the Isle of Wight in 2019. The
first bird was seen for a couple of hours perched on a submerged "island"
in the middle of Ibsley Water, and on its second date, flushed all the gulls
and soared off east. A truly moving experience for all those lucky enough
to have seen either of these birds.

Buzzard   *Buteo buteo*
Frequent and quite common; breeds from time to time.

As with Sparrowhawk, there are no meaningful data to report. Since the recovery of the species in the 1980s, Buzzards have become a daily sight over the area in recent years, with up to a remarkable 32 being counted at once (Aug 14th 2008). Breeding occurs within the area treated by this report, but perhaps not every year.

Barn Owl   *Tyto alba*
A very rare visitor.

The only records available are as follows, but no doubt more used to occur.

1985 Ivy Lane	Jan 31st
1998	Feb 7th-8th
2004	Jan 2nd and 16th-18th; Feb 15th
2012	Aug 27th; Oct 20th
2013	Jan 26th
2013	Mar 17th
2014	Dec 27th

Little Owl   *Athene noctua*
Possibly once resident, now a very rare visitor.

BoH records the species as "probably breeding" in the tetrads including the site, but it is not clear whether this was within the area treated here. More recently, just nine records, scattered throughout the year, and only three since 2000.

1996	Apr 2nd; June 15th
1997	July 12th
1998	Feb 8th

1999	Oct 16th; Dec 31st
2001	Oct 28th
2007	May 25th
2015	Feb 11th

Long-eared Owl   *Asio otus*

A very rare visitor, but possibly overlooked.

One record.

| 2010 Ibsley Water | Dec 26th |

A dusk sighting of a bird emerging from roost, and briefly perching in front of the Lapwing Hide. It is entirely likely that occasional birds winter in the dense, impenetrable willow carr in this part of the site, or indeed elsewhere, although the species is genuinely rare in Hampshire.

Short-eared Owl   *Asio flammeus*

A very rare winter visitor.

Four records, the middle two probably of the same bird.

1981 Ivy Lake	Dec 31st
2011 near Visitor Centre	Nov 3rd and 8th
2018 Ibsley Water	Dec 28th

Tawny Owl   *Strix aluco*

A scarce resident.

Tawny Owls occur not uncommonly in the area treated, especially around the Centre and Snails and Ivy Lanes. Two recent counts of six calling males have been made.

Kingfisher *Alcedo atthis*

A scarce resident and occasional breeder.

The only firm published records of breeding are at Spinnaker Lake in 1983, along Dockens Water in 2007, and two pairs in 2014, but it is very likely that attempts are made most years. Birds are often seen along Dockens Water in spring and summer. In winter, birds are more likely to be encountered away from flowing water, notably along the path between Rockford and Ivy Lakes, or around Snails Lane. The maximum count in recent years appears to have been of seven, on Dec 22nd 2002.

Wryneck *Jynx torquilla*

A very rare passage migrant. Formerly bred in the vicinity.

Two records, the first on a very intriguing date indeed.

1977 Ellingham Lake	July 17th
1995 Somerley Lakes	Oct 3rd

Lesser Spotted Woodpecker *Dryobates minor*

A rare visitor and once regular, now very rare breeder.

Dated records exist from 1992, as follows:

1992	Mar 21st
1995 Somerley Lakes	Apr 14th
2000	Feb 4th; Dec 30th

2001 Somerley Lakes	Apr 8th (when reported as present for the 21st year in succession at the site – but no reports from here since!)
2003	Jan 22nd; Feb 19th
2006	July 10th
2007	Feb 2nd

A status change then occurred in 2008, with 18 records between Jan 12th and Apr 17th, and two on at least five dates. Nest-hole excavation was observed in the woods near the Centre. There were then no further records until 2009 (Jan 7th; ♂, Oct 15th; ♀, Oct 18th), 1-2 (a pair) in Sep 2010, and then an interesting series of reports, indicative of breeding in 2011 a pair was seen regularly and observed drumming and displaying during Jan 5th-Apr 7th. They subsequently nested, raising young. One was heard as late as June 30th. All records came from the area between Ellingham Drove and the south end of Ivy Silt Pond. A male was seen intermittently from Nov 12th-Dec 5th 2012, one was seen on Jan 1st 2013 and one was heard on Feb 25th that year. 2+ were reported on one date in 2016, but the species is now once again very rare or absent, it seems.

Great Spotted Woodpecker   *Dendrocopos major*
A common resident.

Recorded almost daily, with many records from the Centre and Snails Lane, where (among other sites) nests are regularly found.

Green Woodpecker   *Picus viridis*
A common resident.

Green Woodpeckers are frequently to be seen feeding on the lichen heath around the Centre and Goosander Hide, and in other open areas, such as the fields along Snails Lane and the margins of Rockford Lake. They breed regularly in the area, notably at Snails Lane. Seven were noted on Aug 11th 2010, no doubt involving locally fledged birds.

Kestrel   *Falco tinnunculus*
A frequent but perhaps declining visitor.

Again, as with the other "commoner" raptors, meaningful data are hard to come by, but Kestrels are a not infrequent sight over the area, although there is a perception, as in so many areas, of a recent significant decline in numbers.

Red-footed Falcon   *Falco vespertinus*
An extremely rare vagrant from eastern Europe.

One record.
2008 Ibsley Water   2cy ♂, May 18th

Merlin   *Falco columbarius*
A very rare passage and winter visitor.

The data are probably woefully incomplete, but Merlins are plainly genuinely rare at Blashford. These are the only dated records which can be extracted from the database. All fall between Sep 19th and Mar 20th.

1979	Nov 24th
1989	Oct 25th
1990	Jan 21st
1994	Mar 20th; Dec 30th
1996	Jan 6th; Sep 18th
2003	Dec 4th
2004	Jan 22nd; Sep 19th
2005	Jan 23rd
2008	Sep 26th; Nov 18th
2010	Nov 19th
2012	Dec 6th
2013	1, Jan 16th; singles on five dates, Oct 24th-Dec 27th
2015	Feb 1st
2016 Ibsley Water	Nov 10th-11th
2018 Ibsley Water	Mar 7th
2019 Ibsley Water	Nov 9th; Dec 20th
2019 Ivy Lake	Dec 23rd
2020 Ibsley Water	Dec 15th and 19th

Hobby   *Falco subbuteo*

A regular passage migrant, but a recent decline.

Hobbies are a major part of the late spring scene at Blashford these days, but it was not always so. Until the new millennium, records were rather few and far between (but poorly kept). The earliest date appears to be Mar 31st 2012. Since about 2005, a significant pre-breeding gathering, of variable size, has generally occurred over Ibsley Water and elsewhere. Fifteen were present on May 9th 2005, and a record 19 on June 5th 2008. Birds are much scarcer in high summer and autumn, and the latest record appears to be of one on Oct 16th 2009. Since about 2011, spring appearances have become much less frequent – e.g. just 14 records in 2015, and only 8 in 2016.

Peregrine   *Falco peregrinus*
An increasingly frequent visitor.

One "at North Poulner" (assuming that means it occurred within our area) on July 5th 1975 was, at the time, a fairly extraordinary record. Again, data are somewhat patchy, but the next dated record is not until Nov 15th 1980. Since then, Peregrines have increased steadily in their occurrence, and have become annual since the late 1980s. It is not uncommon for (usually single) birds to loaf and hunt around Ibsley Water for several days or even weeks, intermittently. It seems likely that dispersing younger birds are involved, attracted by the large numbers of potential prey items on offer, but kills are rarely noted.

Ring-necked Parakeet   *Psittacula krameri*
A very rare visitor from British feral stocks.

One record.
2008   Aug 21st

This species has yet to establish itself in Hampshire, despite the burgeoning London and north-eastern Surrey populations. It is arguably surprising that it has been found at Blashford at all!

Great Grey Shrike   *Lanius excubitor*
A very rare winter visitor from NE Europe. 3-4 birds.

Given that Great Grey Shrikes winter regularly on the New Forest and adjacent commons, it is perhaps not surprising that the species has occurred at Blashford Lakes, but the records were a long time in coming. In 2010, one was observed on Nov 25th, and then five sightings were made of a single bird between Dec 14th and Mar 17th 2011, no doubt of the bird then regularly using Ibsley Common nearby. A further sighting came on Dec 20th 2011, but not subsequently. Another was seen on Jan 27th 2013.

Jay   *Garrulus glandarius*
A fairly common resident.

Jays are seen year round in small numbers at Blashford Lakes, and there often appears to be an increase in numbers in autumn and early winter.

Magpie   *Pica pica*
A common resident.

Breeds in the area treated, and occasionally forms roosts in willow carr thickets in winter. 44 recorded at roost at North Poulner Lake Dec 27th 2017.

Jackdaw   *Coloeus monedula*
A frequent visitor.

Large numbers are often seen at Ibsley Water, especially on winter evenings. Birds go to roost in the Avon valley and other nearby areas (e.g. Ringwood Forest), but rather few are seen on the ground at Blashford Lakes. Breeds in Snails Lane at least.

Rook   *Corvus frugilegus*
A frequent visitor.

Status as Jackdaw, with rookeries sometimes active along the A338.

Carrion Crow   *Corvus corone*
A common resident.

Commonly seen, but there are no records of substantial numbers.

Raven   *Corvus corax*
A rare but increasing visitor. Recently reestablished as a breeding resident in the immediate area.

Many quite recent records since the first in 1998, with a sharp increase since 2007, reflecting recolonisation of the area as a breeding species in recent years.

1998 Mockbeggar Lake	Jan 18th
1999 Moyles Court	2, Nov 14th; 2 NW, Nov 21st – presumed to relate to the same birds, and to have been in the recording area.

2000	2, Jan 19th
2001	2, Sep 1st; 2 east,
	Dec 2nd
2003	2, Feb 2nd; flew west, Dec 31st
2004	flew east, Jan 11th;
	4, Dec 18th;
2005	Feb 6th
2006	2, Aug 30th; Dec 26th
2007	9 records
2009	2 records
2010	11 records
2011	19 records
2012 onwards	too frequent to have reliable data

In addition, there are many undated records of birds (up to four) flying over Snails Lane, mostly in early spring, and all since 2010). The recent apparent "decline" may simply be due to increased observer familiarity, and thus complacency! The species is seen regularly these days.

Waxwing *Bombycilla garrulus*
A very rare winter visitor from NE Europe.

Seven very recent records, of an unknown number of individuals.

2010	4, Ivy Lake, Dec 18th; 4, Dec 22nd; 11 SW
	over Ivy Lake Dec 27th; 2, Dec 29th
2011 Snails Lane	18, Feb 19th; 6, Mar 5th; 1 Mar 6th

All of the above occurred during the exceptional "irruption" winter of 2010/11.

Coal Tit   *Periparus ater*

An uncommon resident.

Small numbers are regularly recorded, and a few pairs breed in the area treated. A high count of 17 was made on Jan 20th 2007.

Marsh Tit   *Poecile palustris*

A rare visitor, but possibly an incipient breeder.

1994 Ivy Lake	2, Sep 25th and Dec 3rd (same?)
2007	Jan 25th; Nov 17th
2008	Nov 15th-23rd; Dec 31st-Feb 11th 2009 (intermittently)
2010 Ivy Lake	May 1st and 5th, when in song
2017	Jan 14th
2021 Visitor Centre	2, Feb 23rd; 2 (both ringed) present throughout the summer – nuptial behaviour observed; "several" reported (photographed), Sep 1st
2021 Snails Lane	June 24th

Breeding habitat is not lacking, but competition and predation pressures are fierce.

Willow Tit   *Poecile montanus*

A former (apparent) resident.

BoH recorded the species as "possibly breeding" in the relevant tetrad (so it is "on the list"), but there have been no records since.

Blue Tit

Cyanistes caeruleus

A common resident.

Common, conspicuous and a regular breeder around the area.

Great Tit

Parus major

A common resident.

Common, conspicuous and a regular breeder around the area.

Bearded Tit

Panurus biarmicus

A very rare visitor.

Three records, presumed to relate to four individuals.
2010 Ivy Lake   Oct 25th; pair, Dec 5th-26th
2015 Ibsley North Lake   2, Oct 3rd

These records apparently constituted the first for the Avon Valley, at least in the modern era.

Woodlark

Lullula arborea

A rare visitor.

12 records of 22 birds.
1998   Jan 17th
2000 Ibsley Water   flew west, Nov 10th
2006 Ibsley Water   flew west, Oct 10th; 3 over, Oct 21st
2008 Goosander Hide   1-3, Mar 6th-28th; 2, Apr 30th
2009 Rockford Lake   2 over, Oct 22nd
2010 Ibsley Water   Sep 26th

2012 Woodland Hide	♂ in song, Mar 15th
2014 Ibsley Water	4, Sep 1st
2016 Ibsley Water	2, Feb 17th
2017 Ibsley Water	Oct 20th

The series of records of grounded birds in 2008 is intriguing, and suggests the possibility of a future breeding attempt on the more open areas around Ibsley Water, or elsewhere.

Skylark   *Alauda arvensis*

An uncommon passage migrant and winter visitor.

Small numbers of Skylarks are recorded from time to time, notably in autumn and winter, and there are a few records of substantial numbers moving in cold weather (one example is of 2000 on Jan 27th 1979). The species does not breed on site, and is generally quite scarce.

Shore Lark   *Eremophila alpestris*

An extremely rare vagrant.

One record
| 2018 Ibsley Water | Oct 23rd |

One of the most remarkable of all Blashford Lakes records, and only the second ever to have been found inland in the county.

Sand Martin   *Riparia riparia*

An abundant passage migrant and localised breeder.

Sand Martins are the heralds of spring at Blashford, and birds seen there are often the first for the county each year, typically in the second week of Mar, but sometimes earlier. Very large concentrations of passage birds often occur (e.g. 1300, Apr 20th 2006, 1400 (in a snowstorm!), Apr 6th 2008, 3000+, Aug 26th and Sep 10th and 1060, Sep 23rd 2007), usually the largest in the county.

A "large colony" was recorded from 1959, with 500 pairs in 1961, but petered out as the pits were flooded. Ibsley Water was colonised in 1995, and up to 136 pairs bred there until 2000. In 2001, 90 pairs bred at the "new workings", but no more nesting was recorded until 2007, when 15 pairs colonised Ibsley Water once more. Bob Chapman installed artificial nesting pipes in a bank by the Goosander Hide in 2008, and were instantly rewarded by 30 pairs using them that year. In the three subsequent years, 120, 60 and 150 pairs used the facilities at Ibsley Water, with considerable success. The latest record is apparently on Nov 1st 2014.

Swallow *Hirundo rustica*

A common passage migrant and summer visitor.

Swallows are common in spring and autumn, with occasional large gatherings, especially in late Apr-early May (e.g. 3000, Apr 29th 2018; 500-700, May 4th-5th 2012). A few use the Lakes for feeding during the summer, and larger numbers occur again from Aug through to early Oct (all-time record 1500-2000, Sep 10th 2017; also 1010 south, Sep 26th 1999). Currently, no breeding occurs within the area treated. The earliest record appears to be of one on Feb 23rd 2019.

House Martin *Delichon urbicum*

A common passage migrant and summer visitor.

Status much as for Swallow, but with occasional larger counts, e.g. 1500+ Sep 14th 2011, 2000 May 15th 2012 and 7000+ on Sep 11th 2017. A few pairs used to breed on houses within the treated area, but apparently not since 2014.

Cetti's Warbler *Cettia cetti*

A scarce but regular resident.

There is no note of when the first was recorded at Blashford Lakes, but up to four Cetti's Warblers are regularly recorded outside the breeding season. Singing males are regular in suitable breeding habitat, especially at Ivy Lake, especially in

winter and spring. Two territorial males were recorded in 2013, four were in song in late Apr 2017, and eleven were recorded in 2021. Breeding has been proved, after many years of technical uncertainty!

Long-tailed Tit   *Aegithalos caudatus*
A common resident.

Frequently seen throughout the area, and breeds. A remarkable 100 were reported on Oct 31st 1999, spread out in at least five flocks.

Wood Warbler   *Phylloscopus sibilatrix*
A very rare spring passage migrant.

Two records.

| 2007 | singing ♂, Apr 15th |
| 2008 | singing ♂, Apr 25th |

There is no suggestion that these were anything other than passage birds singing briefly on their way to their breeding haunts in the New Forest or elsewhere in Britain. Wood Warblers are almost extirpated in the New Forest, so a repeat is perhaps somewhat unlikely now.

Yellow-browed Warbler   *Phylloscopus inornatus*
A very rare autumn visitor.

Five recent records

2013 Dockens Water	Oct 8th
[2015 near Goosander Hide	Nov 1st – not submitted to HOSRP]
2016	photographed, Oct 10th
2019 Ivy Silt Pond	Jan 8th-29th
2020 Visitor Centre	Jan 30th

2020 Ivy Silt Pond area   Dec 11th-Jan
                                 1st 2021

After the long-predicted first for the
reserve, we did not have to wait long for
the second (although the 2015 bird was
never submitted to HOS). Whether
returning birds are involved we shall never
know. The late 2020 bird is suspected to
have succumbed after a cold spell around
Christmas.

Willow Warbler   *Phylloscopus trochilus*
A common passage migrant, but now a rare breeder.

Common on passage, but much reduced as a breeder: only two pairs were
located in 2021.

Chiffchaff   *Phylloscopus collybita*
A common summer visitor and occasional winter visitor.

Frequently encountered in the summer months. 18 singing males were
noted on Apr 4th 2004. A maximum of eight has been recorded in winter
"proper" (Dec 1995) – 11 on Nov 5th 2020 may have included late migrants.
One described as being one of the forms *abietenus* or possibly *tristis* was at
Spinnaker Lake on Feb 14th and Mar 22nd 1998.

One accepted by HOS as a 'Siberian' Chiffchaff (*P.(c.) tristis*) was near the
Visitor Centre on Jan 21st 2015. Others were suspected on Nov 17th 2013

and Dec 3rd and 5th 2014 (last two possibly the accepted bird above). Another was heard at Ivy Lake on Oct 28th 2017, but HOS (rightly) does not accept 'heard only' records.

Sedge Warbler   *Acrocephalus schoenobaenus*

A scarce passage migrant and very scarce summer visitor. Possibly increasing as a breeder.

Sedge Warblers are inexplicably rare at Blashford Lakes. They are occasionally recorded on passage in very small numbers, but an indication of their scarcity is given by the fact that just five reports were entered

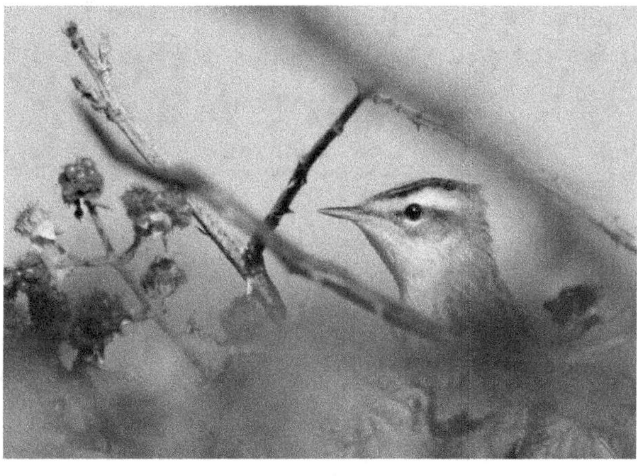

on Going Birding during the whole of 2011! This is perhaps the example par excellence of a species which is not properly reported, and so appears even rarer than it really is, although it may just <u>be</u> very rare. There appears to be plenty of suitable breeding habitat, but they are rare and intermittent breeders. One pair apparently did breed at Ibsley North Lake, until 2009 at least. Three were singing (on and off) near the NE corner of Ibsley Water during April and May 2012. In 2013, 9+ breeding territories were recorded, and in 2014, eight. They appear not to have bred in recent years.

Reed Warbler   *Acrocephalus scirpaceus*
A fairly common passage migrant and summer visitor.

Good numbers of Reed Warblers nest at Blashford Lakes, with males regularly singing even in the tiniest reedbeds. They appear to have colonised in 1986 (two territories at Mockbeggar Lake), and by 2008/9, 18-20 males were in song, rising to 39 in 2013. Significant numbers probably pass through in autumn, but are harder to observe. The latest date on record is Oct 4th 2012.

Grasshopper Warbler   *Locustella naevia*
A very rare passage migrant.

1999	Sep 11th
2007	in song, Apr 16th
2015	July 30th, trapped
2016 Ibsley Water	Aug 6th and 9th – presumed same
2017 Ibsley Water	July 18th, trapped; July 20th, trapped
2018 Ibsley Water	juv, July 21st, trapped

While perhaps more frequent and possibly breeding in the past, "Groppers" are now no more than very rare visitors, although some may well pass through unnoticed in the autumn. The above are the only recent dated records.

Blackcap   *Sylvia atricapilla*

A common passage migrant and summer visitor, with small numbers in winter.

Blackcaps are common in spring and summer. A maximum of 17 territories was recorded in 1986 during Atlas Survey work, and there is no reason to think the total has changed greatly from that level. Up to three have been recorded per day in winter.

Garden Warbler   *Sylvia borin*

A moderately common summer visitor.

Garden Warblers are common in summer, and may be increasing. 13 males were noted in spring 2008 and 2014, rising to 31+ more recently.

Lesser Whitethroat   *Curruca curruca*

A scarce but under-recorded passage migrant. Potential (re)coloniser.

Dated records are very few indeed. This species used to breed in the area (e.g. three territories recorded in 1982), but does not do so today. At least one was recorded in song in 1995 and 1996, but there were no more records until 2002, followed by singles in 2004, 2007 and 2008, all of which were on passage. 2011 produced five birds between Aug 13th and Sep 17th, with three on the later date. Four were in song in May 2020, and another in May 2021.

Whitethroat   *Curruca communis*
An uncommon passage migrant and very scarce summer visitor.

Whitethroats are doubtless under-recorded, but the species does appear to be genuinely quite rare. One singing on Apr 25th 2009 was the Reserve warden's first record of a territorial male. One held territory in May and June 2010, but showed no evidence of having attracted a mate. Only two more were seen that year (both in autumn), but 2011 produced 18 autumn birds, between July 11th and Sep 17th. Other singing males were present on Apr 22nd 2014, Apr 10th-July 3rd 2015 and Apr 24th-25th 2016. A claim of juveniles seen on Sep 5th 2015 might suggest successful breeding, but the male's extended song period that year suggests otherwise. Two territories in 2021 finally included the first proved breeding for the area. 14 have been ringed since 2011, almost all dispersing juveniles.

Dartford Warbler   *Curruca undata*
A very rare visitor.

Four records
2006 Ivy Lake	Oct 13th
2010 Ibsley Water	June 20th
2014 Ivy Lake	juv, Oct 2nd
2015 near Waterworks	Oct 3rd-11th

Another inexplicably scarce species given its relative abundance just a couple of kilometres away, and the known propensity of Dartford Warblers to wander ("migrate" would be too strong) after the breeding season.

Firecrest   *Regulus ignicapilla*

A rare visitor and probable incipient breeder.

About 20 records to 2015, since increased.

1996 Kingfisher Lake	Jan 1st
2004	Nov 29th
2008	Aug 24th; Oct 26th; Nov 20th & Nov 27th; very intermittently, Dec 6th-Feb 27th 2009; two present on two dates
2010	Feb 27th; Nov 2nd & 8th
2011	male on territory reported in HBR
2013	Apr 2nd
2014	Sep 25th
2015	Jan 16th; four records in Feb; 2 in Dec
2016	17 records, in both winter periods – doubtless some duplication (but 5 on Jan 29th)
2017	10 records
post-2017	regular, albeit in very small numbers

Given the recent explosion in the local breeding population (county total of territorial males up to almost 900 in 2016, compared with 47 just fifteen years earlier), yet more records are to be expected.

Goldcrest   *Regulus regulus*

A common resident and passage migrant.

Frequently recorded in small numbers, with a likely autumn passage. 13 on Dec 13th 2014 was a high count. 20 were noted on Sep 26th 2015.

Wren   *Troglodytes troglodytes*

A common resident.

Present year round in good numbers, and breeds widely. 29 territories on the reserve proper in 2016.

Nuthatch   *Sitta europaea*

An uncommon resident.

Small numbers regularly use the Reserve and nearby gardens. It is unclear whether breeding occurs.

Treecreeper   *Certhia familiaris*

An uncommon resident.

Small numbers regularly use the Reserve and nearby gardens. Breeding certainly occurs.

Starling   *Sturnus vulgaris*

A common resident, with numbers supplemented in winter when large roosts sometimes occur. Vast numbers in 2013/14.

Small numbers feed around the area all year, and a few pairs breed. In winter, immigrants boost the population substantially, and large roosting flocks often appear, generally using the reedbeds on Ivy Lake. Recent counts have included 2000 in Oct and Nov 2006, 8000 estimated on Dec 25th 2007, 1500 on Dec 1st 2009, 3000 on Nov 17th 2010 and 5000 on Oct 10th 2011, but no large flocks occurred in 2012. This was well-remedied by events in late 2013, when somewhere between 50,000 and 300,000 roosted near Ellingham Church and were regularly over Ibsley Water.

25,000 were estimated in late 2014. Some 30-40,000 roosted in winter 2019/20, and perhaps 10,000 were present in early 2021.

Song Thrush   *Turdus philomelos*
A common resident.

Birds are present year round, and several pairs breed. 15 territories on the reserve proper in 2016. Light passage is sometimes detected in autumn.

Mistle Thrush   *Turdus viscivorus*
An uncommon resident.

Small numbers are present all year round, and a few pairs probably breed. The record count is of 20 at North Somerley Lake on Oct 28th 2001.

Redwing   *Turdus iliacus*
A common winter visitor.

Present in good numbers in winter, sometimes abundantly in wooded areas, with numbers occasionally boosted by cold weather influxes. The record count is of 200 on Dec 14th 2008.

Blackbird   *Turdus merula*
A common resident.

Present throughout the area, with many breeding pairs, supplemented by autumn migrants and winter visitors. 22 territories on the reserve proper in 2015.

Fieldfare   *Turdus pilaris*

An uncommon winter visitor.

Present in small numbers in winter, with numbers occasionally boosted by cold weather influxes. The record count is of 200 on Nov 28th 2010.

Ring Ouzel   *Turdus torquatus*

A very rare autumn passage migrant.

Four records.

2005	Oct 7th; Oct 23rd
2010	Oct 17th
2015 Ibsley Water/	1cy, Nov 2nd
Mockbeggar Lake	

Latchmore Bottom, just a few kilometres away, is a regular and quite reliable autumn staging post, so we might expect more frequent occurrences at Blashford Lakes, but Ring Ouzels are notoriously highly specific in their choice of stopover localities.

Spotted Flycatcher   *Muscicapa striata*

A rare passage migrant

Whether Spotted Flycatchers used regularly to breed in the area treated is a moot point. There are few published records, but older data for this species (before its fairly recent and serious decline) are aggregated and thus local records are lost. In recent years, it has been a distinctly rare autumn migrant, although a pair feeding well-grown young on Aug 12th 2007 is suggestive of at least fairly local breeding. In the four years 2009-

13, just 2, 3 and 5 birds respectively were noted, between Aug 31st and Sep 17th. 10-20 bird-days were logged in Aug/Sep 2016.

Robin   *Erithacus rubecula*
A common resident.

Common throughout the area, with breeding occurring very widely. 18 territories noted in 2016.

Nightingale   *Luscinia megarhynchos*
A rare passage migrant and former breeder.

BoH records this species as "probably breeding" in the relevant tetrad, and a territory was recorded at Mockbeggar Lake in the 1980s, but Nightingales are now very scarce spring migrants in the area treated. Since 1994, about 19 reports have been submitted, mostly of singing males on one date only, but with series suggestive of territories, if not breeding per se, in 2001 and 2005. None was between Apr 4th 2006 and Aug 11th 2015, when one (a dispersing post breeder) was seen. Most recently, one was in song near the Goosander Hide on Apr 25th 2020.

Pied Flycatcher   *Ficedula hypoleuca*

A very rare passage migrant.

Four records.
2010	Aug 30th
2011	Sep 17th
2016	Apr 25th
2019 Snails Lane	Aug 31st

Black Redstart   *Phoenicurus ochruros*

A very rare late autumn passage migrant.

Three records.
1995 Ibsley Water	Nov 19th
2010 Water Works	Nov 10th
2017 near Ibsley Water	Mar 23rd

Redstart   *Phoenicurus phoenicurus*

An occasional but rare summer and early autumn visitor.

The status of this species is unclear. There are only six dated records of five birds pre-2011, but in 2011 two females/juveniles were by Ivy Silt Pond on June 18th (failed breeders, or dispersing birds from New Forest breeding sites?), two juveniles were present on July 13th, a male was near Ibsley Water on Aug 13th, and at least two were ringed on Aug 15th. In addition, up to two juveniles were just outside the area at Ibsley North Lake during Aug 2011. One was recorded on Sep 27th 2015, and another on Aug 6th 2016. A further two were recorded in Aug 2021.

Whinchat   *Saxicola rubetra*

A very rare passage migrant.

Four records.
2005	Aug 23rd; Sep 25th; Oct 2nd
2009	Sep 13th

Stonechat   *Saxicola rubicola*

A very rare visitor, and possible very occasional breeder.

Given that the species breeds on Ibsley Common, no more than 2km away, and disperses widely to Avon Valley sites in autumn and winter, it seems astonishing that Stonechats appear to be rarer at Blashford Lakes than (for example) Little Stints!

There are only seventeen dated records, all since 1997. Most are of single birds, but five were recorded on Oct 2nd 2005, and a pair was feeding two fledglings at Ibsley North Lake on July 9th 2005.

Wheatear   *Oenanthe oenanthe*

An uncommon passage migrant.

A few are seen in spring (the earliest being two on Mar 17th 2008) and autumn every year, generally no more than two at a time, and usually at Ibsley Water. The maximum count on record is of five on 9th Aug 1996. Of dated recent records, 32 were in spring and 19 were in autumn.

Tree Sparrow   *Passer montanus*

A very rare former resident, not recorded in recent years.

There are reports, little more than anecdotal, of the former occurrence of this species, which has declined to virtual extinction in the county. It is unclear when or how commonly it used to occur. It certainly does not get recorded these days.

House Sparrow   *Passer domesticus*

A very localised resident.

This species is oddly very rare indeed on the Reserve proper, even given the recent establishment of well-stocked feeding stations. The only recent records are of one on Sep 17th 2010, a pair on Apr 23rd and two females on May 31st 2012 (one also on June 2nd). However, they do breed in residential and farming sites in the south of the area, and are frequent and indeed increasing in frequency around Snails Lane.

Dunnock   *Prunella modularis*

A common resident.

Frequent throughout the area, and breeds commonly.

Yellow Wagtail   *Motacilla flava*

A rare passage migrant and former breeder.

Three territories were recorded at Mockbeggar Lake in 1988, and two pairs were at "Blashford" (exact site unknown) as recently as 1994, and it is likely that breeding used to occur quite regularly, especially before (a) the construction of the pits and (b) the near total loss of the species as a breeder in the region as a whole. Nowadays, however, Yellow Wagtails are only rather scarce and probably declining passage migrants. 25 on Aug 31st 2005 was an excellent count, and all more recent records have been of 1-3 birds, mostly in flight. Just one was seen in 2013. Bird-day totals since then are tabulated below

2014	2015	2016	2017	2018	2019	2020
2	2	8-9	7	1	2	0

There appear to be no records of nominate form Blue-headed Wagtails (*M.f.flava*), or indeed any other form of "Yellow" Wagtail than the British *flavissima*.

Grey Wagtail   *Motacilla cinerea*

A resident in small numbers, breeding nearby, or possibly within the area.

A few Grey Wagtails are generally present year-round, especially along the Dockens Water and Rockford Lake, but they do not appear to breed in the area treated here.

Occasional "flyovers" in spring and autumn suggest a light passage, too. A fairly extraordinary 27 were counted at Ibsley North Lake on Aug 8th 2005, no doubt involving dispersing family parties from New Forest streams.

Pied Wagtail   *Motacilla alba*

A common year-round visitor, numbers significantly boosted in autumn and winter. Birds of the continental race ('White Wagtail') occur on passage.

Pied Wagtails are a frequent sight around the Lakes, especially in autumn and winter, and occasionally breed. Significant numbers gather around Spinnaker Lake Sailing Club on autumn and winter evenings, and this appears to be a pre-roost gathering, with most birds, and more besides, heading for roost sites in the north of the Reserve, especially in the willow carr between the Goosander and Lapwing hides. Sample high counts of this roost

include 400 in Dec 1998, 130 on Feb 6th 2000, 200 on Sep 10th 2005, 270 on Nov 22nd 2007 and 220 on Oct 2nd 2012, suggesting that the roost size has been roughly stable over recent years.

White Wagtails (*M.a.alba*) are scarce but regular early spring (and to a lesser extent autumn) migrants, in very small numbers. Following six at Mockbeggar Lake on Apr 23rd 1989 (still the record count), some 65 have been recorded, all between 2006 and 2021, and almost all at Ibsley Water.

Spring birds occurred between Mar 17th and May 21st, and the autumn records were on Aug 27th and Oct 23rd.

Meadow Pipit   *Anthus pratensis*
A regular visitor, mostly in autumn and winter.

A few are generally to be found around Ibsley Water and in rough grassland areas (e.g. Snails Lane fields) in autumn and winter, but only very occasional observations are made in the summer months. Any autumn passage is generally poorly detected, but a record of 101 south and SW over Mockbeggar Lake on Nov 2nd 1991 confirms that such movements do occur from time to time. The all-time high count is of 250 on Mar 20th 2008.

Tree Pipit   *Anthus trivialis*
A rare (or overlooked) autumn migrant.

13 dated records of 21 birds, almost all recent.

1994	Aug 23rd
2007	2, Aug 11th; Sep 1st; Sep 9th
2009 Ibsley Water	Apr 12th; Sep 11th
2010 Snails Lane	Aug 14th
2011	5 trapped, Aug 15th
2012	Sep 2nd; Oct 28th
2013 Ibsley Water	Apr 14th
2016 Visitor Centre	Sep 1st
2017 Ibsley Water	4, Aug 20th

There are further undated records from ringers around Ibsley Water in August.

Water Pipit   *Anthus spinoletta*

A rare winter visitor or passage migrant.

1980	Dec 29th
2004	Apr 10th
2006	Oct 28th
2009 Mockbeggar Lake	Jan 18th; Dec 20th
2010 Ibsley Water	Mar 16th and 26th; Nov 18th & 26th; Dec 5th
2011 Ibsley Water	Jan 1st-6th (all presumed to refer to one wintering bird since Nov 18th 2010); Feb 28th-Mar 2nd; Mar 20th; Oct 30th
2012 Ibsley Water	Jan 25th-27th; Feb 25th; Mar 17th-Apr 10th
2014 Ibsley Water	Mar 27th
2015 Ibsley Water	Mar 18th
2016 Ibsley Water	Mar 22nd; Nov 3rd-Dec 27th
2017 Ibsley Water	22 records of perhaps 3 birds to Apr 1st; another to end of year
2018 Ibsley Water	1-2, Jan-Mar; Oct 25th-year end
2019 Ibsley Water	2 (one same as 2019) Jan 1st; one or other until Mar 28th; Oct 23rd-Nov 12th
2020 Kingfisher Lake	east, Jan 5th
2020 Ibsley Water	Feb/Mar; Oct 15th at least-Dec 18th

March is perhaps the best month to see this species at Blashford, but it appears now to winter in very small numbers, mostly around Ibsley Water.

Rock Pipit   *Anthus petrosus*

A very rare passage migrant/winter visitor.

14 records, all recent, involving perhaps 16 birds.

2005 Ibsley North Lake	July 30th
2008 Ibsley Water	Feb 24th; 2, Mar 7th;
	2, Mar 24th
2011 Ibsley Water	Oct 30th; Nov 8th
2012 Ibsley Water	Mar 17th-18th (considered possibly *littoralis*
	– see below);
	2, Apr 5th
2013 Ibsley Water	Nov 10th
2015 Ibsley Water	Oct 22nd
2016 Ibsley Water	Oct 16th-Nov 6th; another, Oct 19th-23rd
2017 Ibsley Water	Mar 31st

The date of the first is extraordinary! The two on Mar 7th 2008 and the 2017 bird were considered to be Scandinavian Rock Pipits (*A.p.littoralis*). In addition, a bird at Ibsley Water on Mar 19th 2011 was considered by the same experienced and reliable recorder to resemble *littoralis*, rather than Water Pipit, and although the record was not submitted to HOS, it is published here for completeness.

Chaffinch   *Fringilla coelebs*

A common resident, with more in autumn and winter.

Ever present around the area, and quite large concentrations occur at feeding stations in winter. The only concrete count of any note is a pretty extraordinary 600+ flying WNW with a few Bramblings over Snails Lane in half an hour in the afternoon on Mar 3rd 2012. The birds were following a very narrow flight path off the New Forest, with none over Spinnaker Lake at all. While it has been suggested that this was merely a movement to roost, the intensity and strength of the movement does suggest some kind of actual passage.

Brambling   *Fringilla montifringilla*
A variably common winter visitor.

Meaningful records are really only available since about 2007, when substantial winter feeding began, and the species has presumably increased and become more regular. Nevertheless, numbers present vary between winters, and indeed within winters. Large counts have included 100 on Mar 23rd 2008, 80 at the Centre on Feb 25th 2010 and a spectacular 300 on Mar 31st 2011 (a day when a major influx occurred at some other Hampshire sites). All these indicate that peak numbers may well be present during the late winter departure period. Bramblings have regularly used a Snails Lane garden in winter since early 2010 as well, with a maximum of 42 present at once.

Hawfinch   *Coccothraustes coccothraustes*

A very rare visitor.

Fifteen records.

2005	Nov 23rd and 26th; Dec 3rd and 27th
2010	1-2, Dec 10th
2010 Snails Lane	2, Dec 31st
2013 Ibsley Water	Apr 11th
2016 Visitor Centre	Feb 9th
2016 Snails Lane	2, Oct 29th
2017 North Poulner Lake	Nov 18th-Feb 2018
2017 near Goosander hide	Nov 12th; 2, Dec 3rd
2018 Linbrook East Lake	Apr 9th
2019 Ivy Lane	1+, Dec 13th
2020 Mockbeggar Lake	5, Nov 29th
2021 Mockbeggar Lake	4, July 4th

A tantalising record of 30 at Moyles Court in Feb 1975 may have constituted the first record for the area, but whether they strayed west of the Gorley Road is unknown. The bird in scrub habitat in 2017-18 was unprecedented in its long stay. The repeated records of multiple birds at Mockbeggar in 2020 or 2021 may or may not be the start of a trend.

Bullfinch   *Pyrrhula pyrrhula*

An uncommon but quite conspicuous resident.

Bullfinches are notably easy to find at Blashford Lakes. They are recorded on almost any visit to the area between the water treatment plant and Rockford Lakes, an area where many non-native *Prunus* trees and blackthorn bushes grow. They are also commonly found along Snails Lane.

While birds become much more inconspicuous in the spring and summer, they are present year round, and to breed. Two newly-fledged juveniles were ringed on Aug 21st 2011, for instance. Numbers are generally in single figures, but up to 12 have been counted in a single day.

Greenfinch   *Chloris chloris*

A common but nationally declining year round visitor, which presumably breeds.

Despite recent declines, Greenfinches are not uncommon around Blashford Lakes and neighbouring gardens, but they are most conspicuous when roosting, which they still do regularly in laurels just south of Ibsley Water. 150-200 used to gather in trees in that area on most winter evenings, and 300 did just that on Nov 15th 2014. Sadly, numbers have fallen since, in line with national trends.

Linnet   *Linaria cannabina*

A rather scarce visitor.

150 were at Mockbeggar Lake on Apr 30th 1986, but this is by far and away the largest count ever recorded at the site. For example, just three records (of eight birds) were submitted via Going Birding in the whole of 2012! As with other "common" species, a lack of records need not always mean such an extreme lack of birds as the data suggest, but it might. 40 at Ibsley Water on Oct 7th 2017 were very notable, and a large flock of up to 70 was there in mid Dec 2018, growing to 80 in early 2019.

Common Redpoll   *Acanthis flammea*
A rare but fairly regular winter visitor from NE Europe.

About 14 have been recorded, all during 2008-14 and all at the Woodland
Hide, as follows:

2008	Mar 7th-Apr 8th; 2, Nov 18th-Dec 29th (one until Jan 3rd)
2009	Mar 19th; Mar 25th-Apr 13th (see below); 5 more, early April
2011	Jan 9th-Mar 19th
2012	Mar 17th-20th
2014	2, Jan 11th-Mar 27th

This bird has only fairly recently been 'split' from Lesser Redpoll. For a short
period, Common (or Mealy) Redpolls were rare but apparently quite
regular visitors to Blashford Lakes. The second 2009 bird detailed above
showed characteristics of the form *rostrata*, the so-called Greenland
Redpoll, the first and only Hampshire record, and one of very few indeed in
southern England.

Lesser Redpoll   *Acanthis cabaret*
A fairly common passage migrant and winter visitor.

Ones and twos regularly occur in autumn (but flyover migrants also occur
in rather larger numbers, e.g. 45 NE on Nov 2nd 1991). Numbers on the
ground do not generally climb significantly until the new year, when
Redpolls become conspicuous and popular visitors at the Woodland Hide,
and occasionally at other feeding stations. The maximum count appears to
be of about 50 on Dec 15th 2010, when birds were present in small parties

in several areas where they had been absent just the day before. Numbers have been low since about 2014 (*cf.* Common Redpoll above).

Crossbill   *Loxia curvirostra*
A rare visitor, but probably under-recorded.

32 records of at least 104 birds, all recent, and all of birds in flight. Little seasonal pattern.

2003	2, Dec 14th
2006	3, June 23rd; 3, Nov 19th
2007	Jan 1st
2008	11, June 6th; July 3rd; 2, July 12th; 2, July 22nd; 6, July 25th; 6, Oct 26th
2009	2, July 25th
2010	1+, Jan 28th; 2, Oct 23rd; 2, Dec 13th
2011	flock, July 27th; 2+, Sep 28th; 1+, Nov 11th; 3+, Nov 23rd; 2+, Dec 3rd
2012	5+ flew SW, date unknown
2013	4 flew north, Mar 19th; 2, July 15th; 12, Dec 23rd
2014	1 flew over, Dec 6th
2015	7 east, Aug 1st; 12 flew over, Oct 11th
2016	2, Apr 24th; Oct 6th
2017	3+, May 27th
2019	north-west, Jan 12th; Feb 16th; Feb 28th
2020 Snails Lane	west, June 25th
2020 Mockbeggar Lake	2, Nov 29th

Goldfinch   *Carduelis carduelis*
A fairly common year round visitor.

While numbers appear to peak in autumn and early winter, Goldfinches can be seen year round, and are particularly conspicuous in autumn when they feed on thistles and other seed-bearing plants. Whether they breed on site is not known. 100 were counted on Oct 2nd 2005, and 150 at Ibsley Water on Aug 19th 2015.

Siskin   *Spinus spinus*
A common migrant and winter visitor; a few in summer.

Siskins occur quite commonly around the area, but flocks are mercurial and highly mobile. A favoured area is the alder carr just south of the Centre, around the Woodland Hide. The highest count is of 300 on Dec 13th 1999.

Snow Bunting   *Plectrophenax nivalis*
A very rare winter visitor.

One record.
2010 Ibsley Water   2, Dec 5th

Corn Bunting   *Emberiza calandra*
A formerly rare visitor, now absent.

There appear to be none but anecdotal records of this species, which may once have been not uncommon in the area. Sadly, it is now completely lost.

Yellowhammer   *Emberiza citrinella*

A very rare visitor.

Three dated records.

2000 N. Somerley Lake	2, May 6th
2003 Mockbeggar Lane	in song, Nov 30th
2008 Ibsley Water	flew north, Apr 21st

This species may well once have been more common, and is possibly under-reported even today, although it is undoubtedly very scarce, at best.

Cirl Bunting   *Emberiza cirlus*

An extirpated former resident.

Now sadly gone from the county (and indeed the region), Cirl Buntings bred in the relevant tetrad during at least 1961-70, and did so "at Rockford" as late as 1982, and probably in 1983, the last breeding pair ever recorded in the county (*BoH*). While it is not absolutely certain that they bred, or even occurred, within the area treated here, it is surely safe to assume that they at least wandered across the Gorley Road from time to time, and the species is given the benefit of the doubt here.

Reed Bunting   *Emberiza schoeniclus*

A common resident, passage migrant and winter visitor.

About 10-14 territories have been noted in recent years, mostly around Ibsley Water and Ivy Lake, and in winter the species is more widespread and numerous, especially in cold weather e.g. 14 in a Snails Lane garden on two dates in Dec 2010, 21+ Ibsley Water on Dec 29th 2010, 20 at the Woodland Hide, Mar 6th 2016.

Appendix 1:

Putative/hypothetical species

[White-throated Needletail   *Hirundapus caudacutus]*

[One was "obtained" near Ringwood on July 26th or 27th 1879, having been seen (possibly with another) over the River Avon a few days previously (*BoH*). See Pallas's Sandgrouse below for the (somewhat dubious!) rationale for including the record of this long-distance East Asian migrant in this Report.]

[Pallas's Sandgrouse   *Syrrhaptes paradoxus]*

[Seventeen "flew over the River Avon near Ringwood" on June 8th 1888 (*BoH*), a famous invasion year for this near-mythical Central Asian species. There is no evidence whatsoever that they flew over, or even anywhere near the area treated here, and this record is included on the purely personal whim of the author. Pipe dreams must be permitted!]

[Night-heron   *Nycticorax nycticorax]*
[No confirmed records]

[A small heron seen in near total darkness on Apr 23rd 2011, flying west over Rockford and Ivy Lakes, was almost certainly of this species. However, it did not call, and the observer could not, in good conscience, formally submit the record to HOS. It is included here not for completeness, but for reasons of authorial vanity, if he is honest. The exact same scenario was repeated on May 28th 2020, for the same observer, this time over Snails Lane.]

[Rough-legged Buzzard   *Buteo lagopus*]
[No confirmed records in the area treated]

[A record exists of one "at Rockford" on Apr 7th 1962. There is probably no way of knowing whether the bird was inside the area treated here.]

[Red-rumped Swallow   *Cecropis daurica*]
[A putative vagrant]

[One was reported over Ibsley Water on Apr 18th 2016, but has apparently not been submitted to either country or national recorders.]

[Lapland Bunting   *Calcarius lapponicus*]
[A probable very rare migrant from the high Arctic]

[One was reported on Oct 18th 1988 (heard only) by a very experienced observer, who was wise enough to record it only as a "probable".]

<u>Appendix 2: Escapes/hybrids</u>

Fulvous Whistling Duck　　　　　*Dendrocygna bicolor*

Ibsley Water and Ivy Lake, May 10th 2008.

Cackling Goose　　　　　　*Branta hutchinsii*

See Canada Goose account in main systematic list.

Bar-headed Goose　　　　　*Anser indicus*

Recorded 1996, 1999, 2002; Ibsley Water 2003; Ibsley Water, July 2nd and 16th 2005; 6 dates (Jan, July, Sep) in 2007; June/July, Sep/Nov 2009; 1-3, 2010, max 3, Nov; Jan 2nd and Oct 16th 2011; Jan 5th 2015; Jun 10th-July 30th 2018.

Emperor Goose　　　　　*Anser canagicus*

One paired with a Barnacle Goose + 1 hybrid juvenile, Aug 14th 2016; probably same, Sep 17th 2020.

Ross's Goose　　　　　*Anser rossii*

Adult, Ibsley Water, June 20th 2020

Lesser White-fronted Goose　　　　*Anser erythropus*

Spinnaker Lake, Dec 21st 1986; Spinnaker Lake, Dec 31st 1986; July 16th and Nov 26th 2000; Sep 2nd, Nov 26th and Dec 31st 2001.

Black Swan　　　　　*Cygnus atratus*

July 13th 1996; Jun 7th-July 23rd 1997; July 6th-Sep 17th 1998; Apr 17th-Oct 7th 1999 (2 on Oct 6th); 3, Jan 16th 2000; May 6th 2000; Dec 26th-28th 2006; Jan 25th and Mar 8th 2007; Feb 10th 2008; 4-6th Mar 2008; Ibsley

Water, 1-2 on 8 dates, summer 2008; 3rd Jan 2009; July 5th 2009; June 20th, Sep 7th 2010; 2011 - between July 25th and Aug 12th; Oct 25th 2015; 1-2 regularly but intermittently 2019-21.

Ruddy Shelduck *Tadorna ferruginea*

One was seen on Ibsley Water on Nov 26th 2020, shortly before five more appeared in the lower Avon Valley. In summer 2021, one of the above or another was present on Ibsley Water from at least July 19th-31st. While a captive origin is possible, it is perhaps at least a likely (especially for the 2021 bird) that records derive from the feral Dutch population. Significant numbers of Ruddy Shelducks were seen in Britain during summer 2021. Analysis and a BBRC/BOURC review are awaited, but many Hampshire and Blashford listers went to see the 2021 bird for 'insurance' purposes!

Muscovy Duck *Cairina moschata*

4, North Poulner Lake, Oct 29th 1995 into 1996.

Wood Duck *Aix sponsa*

Mockbeggar Lake, ♀, Jan 1st 1993.

Maned Duck *Chenonetta jubata*

Ibsley Water, Dec 26th-28th 2006; Jan 14th 2007.

Ringed Teal *Callonetta leucophrys*

Linbrook Lake, Feb 1st 1992; Nov 21st and Dec 5th 1993; Dec 11th 1994; Ivy Lake, Oct 31st 2007; pair, Ibsley Water, Oct 9th 2010.

[Australasian Shoveler]   [*Spatula rhynchotis*]

[A bird reported as apparently resembling the New Zealand form *variegata*, was on Ibsley Water during early 2010, but the observer is now of the view that the bird was more probably a hybrid, possibly a Northern Shoveler x Cinnamon Teal.]

Chiloe Wigeon   *Mareca sibilatrix*

Mockbeggar Lake, May 14th-21st 1994; Mockbeggar Lake, May 31st-July 2nd 1995; Snails Lake, Sep 14th 1996; Ibsley Water, Dec 30th 2001; Ibsley Water, Mar 3rd, Sep 15th and Dec 28th 2002; pair, Ibsley Water, Dec 8th 2007.

Tufted Duck x Pochard hybrids

"Lesser Scaup" type   *Aythya fuligula x farina*

The only dated records are from Ibsley Water from Mar 23rd-Apr 11th 2013, and Nov 18th 2019.

"Greater Scaup type"   *Aythya fuligula x marila*

A male, June 9th-12th 2016

Tufted Duck x Red-crested Pochard hybrid
Aythya fuligula x Netta rufina

One very handsome drake was on Linbrook West in Mar 2020.

Great Bustard   *Otis tarda*

2 flew north, Snails Lake, 22nd Dec 2010.

Greater Flamingo   *Phoenicopterus roseus*

1 flew over Mar 22nd 1998; Ibsley Water, Sep 16th 2011.

Saker Falcon   *Falco cherrug*

One with jesses, Oct 20th 2014

Cockatiel   *Nymphicus hollandicus*

Aug 29th 1997; Sep 17th 2007.

Appendix 3

Look to the future: what's still to come?

This is a question for those long, birdless winter evenings: which species have not yet occurred, but which we might reasonably, if very optimistically, hope for in the future? Since the first edition of this book, no fewer than five of my original top ten have fallen: (2) Glaucous Gull, (3) Lesser Scaup, (4) Red-necked Phalarope, (7) Yellow-browed Warbler and (10) Bonaparte's Gull! A further four "lower" predictions have occurred (Eider; Purple Heron; Little Auk; White-tailed Eagle), and Thayer's (Iceland) Gull and Siberian (Common) Chiffchaff (potential splits) have also been recorded. Here's an updated personal top ten, in very rough order of probability! I have limited myself to birds already on the Hampshire list:

1)	**Shag**	STILL surely long overdue?
2)	**Red-rumped Swallow**	May, Ibsley Water, I reckon.
3)	**Night-heron**	Possibly already recorded!
4)	**Blue-winged Teal**	September, from the Tern Hide.
5)	**Laughing Gull**	Gull species #16 awaits....
6)	**Alpine Swift**	One late March morning...
7)	**Hoopoe**	April, on the lichen heath?
8)	**Montagu's Harrier**	Or will Pallid occur first?
9)	**Penduline Tit**	November, Lapwing Silt Pond.
10)	**Sabine's Gull**	....after a storm

Or failing that lot, here's the rest of my shopping list: **Quail**; **Stone-curlew**; **Squacco Heron**; **Black Stork**; **Pied-billed Grebe**; **Rough-legged Buzzard**; **Spotted Crake**; **Common Crane**; **Dotterel**; **American Golden Plover**; **White-rumped Sandpiper**; **Baird's Sandpiper**; **Spotted Sandpiper**; **Lesser Yellowlegs**; **Gull-billed Tern**; **Caspian Tern**; **Bee-eater**; **Golden Oriole**; **Marsh Warbler**; **Citrine Wagtail**; **Little Bunting**

And finally some really long shots: **Bufflehead**; **Redhead**; **American Bittern**; **American Coot**; **Bridled Tern**.....why not?!?

The Complete Blashford Lakes List

240 BOURC category A and C species have been proved to have occurred in a wild state at Blashford Lakes.

A further four are strongly suspected or recorded as "probables", but with insufficient evidence for firm acceptance.

Species (and one rare subspecies) which were BBRC rarities at the time of their first record (17) are **emboldened**; those which are *still* official national rarities (6) are further **underlined**.

Brent Goose, **Red-breasted Goose**, Canada Goose, Barnacle Goose, Snow Goose, Greylag Goose, Pink-footed Goose, Tundra Bean Goose, White-fronted Goose, Mute Swan, Bewick's Swan, Whooper Swan, Egyptian Goose, Shelduck, Mandarin Duck, Garganey, Shoveler, Gadwall, Wigeon, **American Wigeon**, Mallard, Pintail, Teal, **Green-winged Teal**, Red-crested Pochard, Pochard, **Ferruginous Duck**, **Ring-necked Duck**, Tufted Duck, Scaup, **Lesser Scaup**, Eider, Velvet Scoter, Common Scoter, Long-tailed Duck, Goldeneye, Smew, Goosander, Red-breasted Merganser, Ruddy Duck, Pheasant, Red-legged Partridge, Nightjar, Swift, Cuckoo, Rock Dove/Feral Pigeon, Stock Dove, Woodpigeon, Turtle Dove, Collared Dove, Water Rail, Moorhen, Coot, Little Grebe, Red-necked Grebe, Great Crested Grebe, Slavonian Grebe, Black-necked Grebe, Oystercatcher, **Black-winged Stilt**, Avocet, Lapwing, Golden Plover, Grey Plover, Ringed Plover, Little Ringed Plover, Kentish Plover, Whimbrel, Curlew, Bar-tailed Godwit, Black-tailed Godwit, Turnstone, Knot, Ruff, Curlew Sandpiper, Temminck's Stint, Sanderling, Dunlin, Little Stint, Pectoral Sandpiper, **Long-billed Dowitcher**, Woodcock, Jack Snipe, Snipe, Red-necked Phalarope, Grey Phalarope, **Collared Pratincole**, Common Sandpiper, Green Sandpiper, Redshank, Wood Sandpiper,

Spotted Redshank, Greenshank, Kittiwake, Black-headed Gull, **<u>Bonaparte's Gull</u>**, Little Gull, **<u>Franklin's Gull</u>**, Mediterranean Gull, Common Gull, Ring-billed Gull, Great Black-backed Gull, Glaucous Gull, Iceland Gull (includes *thayeri*), Herring Gull, Caspian Gull, Yellow-legged Gull, Lesser Black-backed Gull, Sandwich Tern, Little Tern, Common Tern, Arctic Tern, **<u>Whiskered Tern</u>**, **White-winged Black Tern**, Black Tern, Arctic Skua, Long-tailed Skua, Little Auk, Red-throated Diver, Black-throated Diver, Great Northern Diver, Leach's Petrel, Fulmar, **White Stork**, Gannet, Cormorant, **Glossy Ibis**, Spoonbill, Bittern, **Cattle Egret**, Grey Heron, Purple Heron, **Great White Egret**, Little Egret, Osprey, Honey-buzzard, Sparrowhawk, Goshawk, Marsh Harrier, Hen Harrier, Red Kite, **Black Kite**, White-tailed Eagle, Buzzard, Barn Owl, Little Owl, Long-eared Owl, Short-eared Owl, Tawny Owl, Kingfisher, Wryneck, Lesser Spotted Woodpecker, Great Spotted Woodpecker, Green Woodpecker, Kestrel, **Red-footed Falcon**, Merlin, Hobby, Peregrine, Ring-necked Parakeet, Great Grey Shrike, Jay, Magpie, Jackdaw, Rook, Carrion Crow, Raven, Waxwing, Coal Tit, Marsh Tit, Willow Tit, Blue Tit, Great Tit, Bearded Tit, Woodlark, Skylark, Shore Lark, Sand Martin, Swallow, House Martin, Cetti's Warbler, Long-tailed Tit, Wood Warbler, Yellow-browed Warbler, Willow Warbler, Chiffchaff, Sedge Warbler, Reed Warbler, Grasshopper Warbler, Blackcap, Garden Warbler, Lesser Whitethroat, Whitethroat, Dartford Warbler, Firecrest, Goldcrest, Wren, Nuthatch, Treecreeper, Starling, Song Thrush, Mistle Thrush, Redwing, Blackbird, Fieldfare, Ring Ouzel, Spotted Flycatcher, Robin, Nightingale, Pied Flycatcher, Black Redstart, Redstart, Whinchat, Stonechat, Wheatear, Tree Sparrow, House Sparrow, Dunnock, Yellow Wagtail, Grey Wagtail, Pied Wagtail, Meadow Pipit, Tree Pipit, Water Pipit, Rock Pipit, Chaffinch, Brambling, Hawfinch, Bullfinch, Greenfinch, Linnet, Common Redpoll, Lesser Redpoll, Crossbill, Goldfinch, Siskin, Snow Bunting, Corn Bunting, Yellowhammer, Cirl Bunting, Reed Bunting

The stunning cover image of a drake Gadwall was taken by **Carl Chapman** of **Wildlife Tours and Education**: (www.wildlifetoursandeducation.co.uk)

WT&E offers widlife and birding tours, photography workshops and corporate events, based in Norfolk.

The modern aerial photos were taken by **Keith Betton**, Hampshire County Bird Recorder.

The historic aerial photos were taken by Mike Read. He has a vast array of wildlife and landscape photos available through his superb website (www.mikeread.co.uk)

About the author: Simon Woolley has lived in Blashford since 2010. His first "Blashford megas" were Smew, Barn Owl, Ring-necked Duck and Black-necked Grebe on a cold day in early 1985. He has personally added Bearded Tit, Glaucous Gull and Long-eared Owl to the Blashford list, and has managed to see 185 of the birds in this book at Blashford, including 123 in, over or from his garden.

Additional photo credits

Bob Chapman: Scaup, Great White Egret, Cormorant, Long-billed Dowitcher, Black-tailed Godwit, Iceland Gull, Ring-billed Gull, Yellow-browed Warbler

Richard Ford: Caspian Gull

Chris and Sue Massie-Taylor: Little Ringed Plover, Redshank, Kingfisher, Sand Martin, Cetti's Warbler, Reed Warbler, Robin, Grey Wagtail, Pied Wagtail

Clear Inner Vision: Cuckoo

My sincere thanks to these photographers.

Other images by the author and Julia Casson

All photos were taken at Blashford Lakes.

INDEX